Souvenirs of Irish Footprints Over Europe

✦

CLASSICS OF IRISH HISTORY

General Editor: Tom Garvin

Original publication dates of reprinted titles are given in brackets

P. S. O'Hegarty, *The Victory of Sinn Féin* (1924)
Walter McDonald, *Some Ethical Questions of Peace and War* (1919)
Joseph Johnston, *Civil War in Ulster* (1913)
James Mullin, *The Story of a Toiler's Life* (1921)
Robert Brennan, *Ireland Standing Firm* and *Eamon de Valera* (1958)
Mossie Harnett, *Victory and Woe: The West Limerick Brigade in the War of Independence*
Padraig de Burca and John F. Boyle, *Free State or Republic? Pen Pictures of the Historic Treaty Session of Dáil Éireann* (1922)
Arthur Clery, *The Idea of a Nation* (1907)
Standish James O'Grady, *To the Leaders of Our Working People*
Michael Davitt, *Jottings in Solitary*
Oliver MacDonagh, *Ireland: The Union and its Aftermath* (1977)
Thomas Fennell, *The Royal Irish Constabulary: A History and Personal Memoir*
Arthur Griffith, *The Resurrection of Hungary* (1918)
William McComb, *The Repealer Repulsed* (1841)
George Moore, *Parnell and His Island* (1887)
Charlotte Elizabeth Tonna, *Irish Recollections* (1841/47 as *Personal Recollections*)
Standish James O'Grady, *Sun and Wind*
John Sarsfield Casey, *The Galtee Boy: A Fenian Prison Narrative*
William and Mary Ann Hanbidge, *Memories of West Wicklow: 1813–1939* (1939)
A. P. A. O'Gara, *The Green Republic* (1902)
William Cooke Taylor, *Reminiscences of Daniel O'Connell* (1847)
William Bruce and Henry Joy, *Belfast Politics* (1794)
Annie O'Donnell, *Your Fondest Annie*
Joseph Keating, *My Struggle for Life* (1916)
John Mitchel, *The Last Conquest of Ireland (Perhaps)* (1858/9)
Harold Begbie, *The Lady Next Door* (1912)
Eugene Davis, *Souvenirs of Irish Footprints Over Europe* (1889)

Souvenirs of Irish Footprints Over Europe

✦

EUGENE DAVIS

edited by Owen McGee

UNIVERSITY COLLEGE DUBLIN PRESS
Preas Choláiste Ollscoile Bhaile Átha Cliath

First published 1889
This edition first published by University College Dublin Press 2006

ISBN 1-904558-53-4
978-1-904558-53-8
ISSN 1393-6883

University College Dublin Press
Newman House, 86 St Stephen's Green
Dublin 2, Ireland
www.ucdpress.ie

Cataloguing in Publication data available
from the British Library

Typeset in Ireland in Ehrhardt by Elaine Shiels
Bantry, Co. Cork
Text design by Lyn Davies,
Frome, Somerset, England
Printed on acid-free paper in England by Athenæum Press Ltd

CONTENTS

INTRODUCTION

Owen McGee

EUGENE DAVIS: A BIOGRAPHICAL NOTE

Eugene Davis was a journalist and one of the best-known Irish popular poets of the Parnell era. Born in Clonakilty, County Cork on 23 March 1857, he came from a well-established family that, since the mid-eighteenth century, had produced many schoolteachers and priests in west Cork. He was the only child of Ellen Davis (Murphy), the second wife of John Davis, a man renowned in west Cork as a teacher of classics and as a tutor to the sons of the local gentry. One of Eugene's stepbrothers, Father Charles Davis (1829–92), achieved brief fame during the late 1880s for his innovative work (with the patronage of a local noble lady) to develop the fishing industry in southwest Cork. His other stepbrother, Frank, was a schoolteacher, while his stepsisters Angela and Fanny married a New York banker and a Skibbereen businessman respectively.[1]

Although he had quite a few friends in west Cork, Eugene probably did not have a close relationship with his family, his siblings being a whole generation older than himself. His father provided him with sound training in the classics, French, German and English literature, and intended him to follow in his uncle's and stepbrother's footsteps by becoming a priest. By his mid teens, however, he had effectively decided instead to enter what he described as 'the glorious guild of journalism, which is ranked as one of the fine arts abroad'. At his father's bidding he studied at the Irish Colleges in Louvain and Paris from 1878 to 1880, but he did not take his ecclesiastical studies very seriously. Already an extremely well-read young man, Davis essentially treated his time in university merely as an opportunity to visit the continent and widen his experience of life. Between 1876 and 1880, writing exclusively under the pseudonym 'Owen Roe', he contributed lengthy series of articles on Irish literary and historical matters almost on a weekly basis, as well as much original verse, to the *Shamrock*, one of Ireland's few literary magazines of note. These very youthful contributions were successful enough to convince him to live henceforth by his pen.

After quitting his ecclesiastical studies for good during 1880, Davis resolved to remain in Paris, settling almost permanently at a hotel on the Rue Saint-Honoré and working as a freelance journalist for both Irish and French newspapers. He adjusted to life in the French capital mostly with the help of Patrick and Joseph Casey, two brothers who lived off income acquired by the sale of family property in Kilkenny city. They nominally worked by day as compositors for the *Galignani's Messenger*. Many years later, Joseph Casey would perform the same service for James Joyce as he had for Davis when he first arrived in the French capital.[2]

During the 1870s and 1880s, Paris served as a kind of second home for several bohemian Irish Catholic *littérateurs*, including John Augustus O'Shea, Edmund O'Donovan, George Sigerson and John Savage; all of whom, like Davis, wrote for the *Irishman*, a radical paper first edited by Denis Holland and later by the disreputable figure of Richard Pigott, or else for the *Shamrock*, a subsidiary publication. Through his connection with the *Irishman* and the Casey brothers (nephews of the mother of the IRB founder James Stephens), Davis came to know many Irish republicans. It is unclear whether or not he ever became a member of the IRB, but he was intensely nationalistic from an early age and clearly republican (although not anti-clerical) in his general political attitude. His sympathies are perhaps best summed up in a very early essay he wrote on the playwright and poet Sheridan Knowles, when he argued that

> All lovers of freedom will find in Knowles's poetry passages which they will revere, for the outspoken sentiments which they embody. Not that slavish love for the so-called Liberalism, often mistaken for liberty; nor yet for those levelling communistic doctrines that find birth in the secret dens of continental cities. No – it was something intermediate – a real independence without the addition of socialism – commingled with a hatred of oppression wherever he met it on his path.[3]

Davis was not a political journalist but in January 1882 he was persuaded by Patrick Egan, the treasurer of the recently suppressed Land League, to become 'acting editor' of a Parisian edition of *United Ireland*, the league's mouthpiece, which had been outlawed in Dublin.[4] This was published for only six weeks, since Dublin Castle prevented its importation into Ireland, but this episode was sufficient to make Davis's name odious to British intelligence. Consequently, he was made the innocent victim of numerous plots.

During 1882–3, while he was editing the recollections of James Stephens and arranging their publication in serial form in the *Irishman* and the *Weekly Freeman*, Davis was targeted by an *agent provocateur*, 'Red' Jim McDermott. When this failed to produce a result, he was subject to the intrigues of Caroll Tevis, a British agent who had managed to get himself appointed as the Parisian envoy of the 'United Irishmen of America', a small revolutionary organisation in New York. Tevis attempted to manipulate Davis and Patrick Casey, who were both Parisian correspondents of the New York *United Irishman* (the nominal organ of the United Irishmen of America), into unwittingly assisting the British secret service's plans. As it was well known in England that many of the funds of the Land League were formerly held in Paris (the reputed home of many a revolutionary grouping), Tevis, Chester Ives, editor of the *Morning News* (Paris), and Richard Pigott (now in the pay of unscruplous Tory agents) published propaganda claiming the existence of an Irish terrorist group in Paris in an attempt to convince the British voting public that Parnell's 'Parisian paymasters' were associated with those (Irish-American) revolutionary fanatics who had planted bombs in the London Underground. At Tevis's request, Casey (though not Davis) gave press interviews expressing some moral support for the 'dynamite war', unaware that in so doing he was acquiring the reputation in the British tabloid press as being the leader of a (non-existent) gang of Irish terrorists. In February 1885, following the planting of a bomb at Westminster by Irish-American extremists, the British government managed to persuade a weak French prime minister to expel all the supposed Irish terrorists from the country. Due to their association with Casey, Davis and the long retired IRB founder James Stephens were expelled from France, although curiously Casey himself does not seem to have been expelled (Davitt suspected that Casey was in British pay). Both Stephens and Davis were allowed to return to France following the collapse of Jules Ferry's government in May 1887, but in January 1889 Davis's name would again be at the centre of controversy, owing to his past association with *United Ireland* (Paris). While breaking up under pressure of interrogations before the Times Commission, Pigott claimed that Davis, as the former editor of *United Ireland*, had letters of Patrick Egan proving that Parnell had supported the Phoenix Park murders. Davis, who was hurt deeply by Pigott's treachery, immediately denied this ridiculous allegation publicly and then assisted Egan and Davitt in compiling information to bring about the infamous forger's downfall.[5]

Between 1885 and 1887 Davis travelled the continent, worked for a time as a correspondent for Irish-American papers like John Boyle O'Reilly's *Pilot* (Boston) and the *Chronicle* (San Francisco), and he was also associated with *La Nouvelle Revue.* This was a French political and literary journal of moderate republican or, perhaps more correctly, Bonapartist-Boulangerist sympathies. Its proprietor and editor was Juliette Adam who was a friend or patron of some of the greatest French writers of the century, such as Gustave Flaubert and Emile Zola, and was renowned for her great beauty and Anglophobia. At Adam's request, Davis wrote several journal-length articles (in French) for the *Nouvelle Revue*, appealing for French support for the cause of Irish independence in terms designed to capture the French popular imagination, while generally supporting the paper's pro-Russian and anti-British editorial stance. He also emphasised the two countries' supposed cultural links.[6] Through a lover and her friendship with Caroll Tevis (who was also watching Adam owing to her Russian political contacts), Maud Gonne would soon become associated with these same circles surrounding Adam, whom she may well have adopted as a personal model in championing her more histrionic brand of nationalist propaganda. Madame Blatavasky, the founder of several theosophical societies and future guru of Yeats's circle, was also a close associate of Adam during the mid-1880s. During the time Davis was a contributor to the *Nouvelle Revue*, it was publishing work by immensely popular French writers of the 1880s, such as the great realist short-story writer Guy de Maupassant and the now generally forgotten figure of Catulle Mendès, a Jewish patron of the arts whose short-lived attempts to create a self-consciously 'decadent' school of writing attracted some international critical attention during the later nineteenth century, and evidently inspired Davis to put together a little poem entitled 'A Love Lay', which he described as being 'paraphrased from the French of Catulle Mendès'.[7]

By the mid-1880s, Davis's writings, although always erudite, had acquired a more graceful and mature style, as well as something of a Francophile bias. His earliest literary contributions to the *Shamrock*, by contrast, were sometimes almost violent in their rhetoric, mostly as a result of his nationalist fervour. Overtly religious passions featured in many of early writings and poems as well, even if his 'Mysteries of the Grave' expressed some doubts as to the possibility of an after-life:

> Living our nine months' lonely life,
> Pent up in this earth's dark womb:
> Destined waifs shall we ever
> thus grope in the rayless night,
> and not see Light?[8]

By the mid-1880s, his religiosity and apparent preoccupation with death became far less pronounced in his verse as he began writing chivalrous love poetry as well as songs on various topical Irish themes. These appeared chiefly in papers such as *United Ireland*, the *Nation*, Cork *Examiner* and the Boston *Pilot*, and many were collected in *A Vision of Ireland and Other Poems*, published in Dublin by Sealy, Bryers & Walker in 1889, the only published volume of his verse. Davis was essentially a romantic poet, deeply attached to nature, but the majority of the hundred-odd poems he wrote for the Irish press between 1876 and 1890 were impersonal 'Young Ireland' style ballads either on Irish history or expressing opposition to British rule. Writing seditious ballads was something he believed was natural for any Irish poet, on the grounds that

> Liberty and song are twin sisters; and he is an unnatural poet who, while he revels in the delights of the one, is not a thorough believer in the justice of the other. They are inseparably united.[9]

Essentially, though, Davis was one of many Irish poets of his generation who did not draw sufficiently upon their own personal experiences for inspiration to develop, or express, their talents fully. He was far more effective as a prose writer (journalism was his sole source of livelihood), though his verse, if rarely of any great symbolical meaning or depth, could often be appealing in its directness and simplicity. One obituarist described him as having been 'Ireland's sweetest singer'.[10]

During the summer of 1887 he returned to Paris and, with the support of General James Dyer MacAdaras, a French general of Irish descent soon to be a moderate republican member of parliament, attempted to set up a bilingual (French and English) Irish nationalist newspaper with himself as editor.[11] When this project fell apart, he moved to Dublin, received employment as an assistant literary editor with the *Nation* and began attending Irish literary societies quite frequently. These included the Pan-Celtic Literary Society in Dublin (which published a tribute of his in verse to Walt Whitman),[12] the Young Ireland Society in Cork and the Southwark Irish Literary Society in London.[13]

Davis was a friend of John O'Leary, had contributed to T.W. Rolleston's *Dublin University Review* and identified with the idea of the existence of a 'Celtic literature',[14] but he does not appear to have associated himself with the emerging Anglo-Irish literary movement. He did, however, essentially prefigure some of Yeats's viewpoints in his early *Shamrock* series, 'Hours with Irish Poets', protesting that compendiums of the work of Irish poets or writers were not being published, and that many Irish writers were being starved of belief in their own creative talents because London book publishers' complete monopoly of the Irish book market was forcing them to conform entirely to English tastes in order to get published.[15] He repeated this argument in *Reliques of John K. Casey, 'Leo'* (Dublin, 1878), a critical biography and compendium of Casey's poems and essays (both published and unpublished) that was commissioned by Casey's widow and remained in print for about five years. Davis prefaced the collection by stating that he had 'no intention of holding up "Leo" as a great poet', but he believed that it was only some kind of mental perversity that prevented many people from acknowledging that, contrary to what English critics had claimed, Casey was capable of writing some pieces of 'sterling merit' upon Irish themes, and had the capacity to develop into a much greater talent had he not died aged just 24. Overall, though, Davis classified Casey's work as being of similar merit to that of minor Young Ireland poets like Richard D'Alton Williams, Thomas D'Arcy McGee and 'the rest of that ilk'.[16]

In the summer of 1890, Davis was dismissed from the staff of the struggling *Nation* (which folded some months later) and, after a brief stay in Paris, left permanently for the United States. Few details are known of his life in America. It appears that he worked for the Chicago *Citizen* and Boston *Pilot*, contributed to several American literary magazines, married into the family of Charles Graham Halpine (an Irish-born, popular American poet), had two daughters, secured an editorial position with an Irish-American paper and was preparing a novel[17] but then he died suddenly in his Brooklyn home on 25 November 1897 at the age of forty, an event that came as a complete shock to his few relatives and friends, as he had always been a very big man of seemingly robust health. Although the Boston *Pilot* claimed that Davis would 'long be remembered as a patriot, poet and an excellent citizen' and the Cork *Examiner* claimed that he could eventually have achieved great fame had he not died so young, Davis appears to have been quickly forgotten in both Ireland and Irish-America, though D. J. O'Donoghue would take care to include an entry on him in *The Poets of Ireland* (1912).[18]

As Davis blossomed as a writer while living on the continent, his writings often had little or nothing in common with those of better-known Irish Catholic writers of the era, such as Charles Kickham or Canon Sheehan. Meanwhile his refined literary style was essentially a perfection of that balance between intellectualist and populist sensibilities which so many better-known Irish nationalist journalists of the Parnell era, most notably his fellow Corkman William O'Brien, strove in vain to attain. These qualities helped to make Davis one of the most fascinating Irish journalists of the Parnell era and enlivened the pages of his most substantial work, *Souvenirs of Irish Footprints Over Europe* (Dublin, 1889), a work of learning, wit, anecdotes and contemporary social observation which is fully imbued with the adventurous spirit of the decade in which it was written.

SOUVENIRS OF IRISH FOOTPRINTS OVER EUROPE AND NOTE ON THE TEXT

Souvenirs first appeared during 1888 in serial form in the *Evening Telegraph* before being republished early the following year in book form by the paper's parent publication, the *Freeman's Journal.* Originally divided into thirty chapters and amassing well over 100,000 words, for a number of reasons it is republished here in a considerably edited format.

Although *Souvenirs* was essentially a tourist guide and personal travelogue, Davis made frequent diversions in his text to give exhaustive accounts of various historic European battles involving Irish-born soldiers. In his treatment of the Irish Colleges, Davis drew upon his own original research and experiences, but his writings on military matters (including the 1798 rebellion) were clearly drawn from the work of other authors. As this derivative material has no intrinsic value in its own right and distracts from the book's main purpose, it has been decided to omit these sections from the text. This has necessitated the deletion of a few chapters, as well as sections of some other chapters. As a result, in a couple of instances, it was found necessary to resequence slightly the order in which the text appears. To create a greater sense of thematic balance in the book, it has been decided to amalgamate the original thirty short chapters into three more lengthy chapters, dealing with Belgium, France and then the rest of Europe. The present ending differs very slightly from the original. The book's original preface, which explained the 'moral' to his tale, has here been merged with his brief concluding remarks at the end of the original text to form a new conclusion.

The chief merit of Davis's book lies not in his abilities as an historian – his imagination and writing style are far too colourful for that – but rather in his own anecdotes and socio-political observations about life on the continent. These provide us with a fresh insight into the social and cultural attitudes of Irish nationalists of his day, as well as a good inkling as to how contemporaries perceived Ireland's relationship with the European continent during the 1880s, a decade in which the future shape of Irish political society was in many senses being forged and when an optimism abounded that Ireland itself was about to become one of the nation states of Europe for the first time. These qualities help to make *Souvenirs* not only an entertaining and informative read, but also a work of much historical interest and relevance.

A noticeable trait in Davis's book is his attempt to be as balanced as possible in his judgments of the virtues, or vices, of various classes in society. This is not surprising. Although his own political predilection was for republicanism, he is writing here for an audience whose political sympathies were more conservative than his own, since the *Freeman's Journal* had a predominantly upper-middle-class and Catholic readership. This is reflected by the fact that Davis assumes that his readers could afford to go on European holidays and send their children to prestigious private schools on the continent. Indeed, Davis even goes so far as to provide assessments of the quality of various educational institutions to advise wealthy Irish Catholic families whether or not they should send their children abroad to be educated. Meanwhile his discussions of church history and the manuscript archives in several continental libraries would indicate that his book was aimed partly at a scholarly audience, including potential priests. Despite this fact, however, Davis takes care not to lose the 'common touch' in most of his anecdotes, as illustrated by his colourful accounts of village fairs, crank tour-guides, petty thieves, Cockney tourists, Parisian cafes, music halls or women's fashions. His republican sympathies become particularly clear in his treatment of Daniel O'Connell and the French revolution, but this rebellious tenor of his writings is quickly moderated thereafter by his entirely positive portrayal of the administrators of the various Irish Colleges, his generally negative comments on continental socialist revolutionaries, and his (slightly) sympathetic portrayal of former members of the Irish Catholic landed gentry, now living in exile in Rome.

Self-conscious of his status as a *littérateur*, Davis subscribes very much to the view that 'the aristocracy of talent' is 'the only aristocracy worthy of the name'. He brings such sensibilities to bear in his remarkably vivid and frequently amusing vignettes of various political, literary and religious figures that appear in the text. His predilection for the company of women adds colour to his judgments of various social issues and, indeed, his generally idealistic attitude to women, or professed admiration for 'the perfections of the sex', adds as well to the book's humour value.

Davis's account of the history of the Irish community in Paris – of which he himself is a part – is curiously impersonal, but nevertheless valuable. If his portraits of various obscure or forgotten figures are fascinating in themselves, his pen pictures of well-known historical figures are enlivened by the fact that many of these individuals were still alive, or in living memory, when this book was written. For example, he provides some incidental information which reveals how memories of the United Irish rebels and members of the Irish Legion in the Napoleonic army were preserved in Paris as recently as the late nineteenth century.

As a former ecclesiastical student in Louvain and Paris, Davis's treatment of the now mostly defunct Irish Colleges on the continent is also interesting. Many students of Irish history today (as in Davis's own time) are familiar with the history of these institutions when they were at their peak during the seventeenth or eighteenth centuries, but Davis also discusses their status in his own day. Such material helps enliven his descriptions of 'Irish footprints' in countries such as Italy and Spain, where his capacity for making social observations was limited by the fact that he did not live in these countries for any length of time.[19] Finally, his account of Irishmen in the armies or diplomatic corps of central Europe is disappointingly brief, but nonetheless interesting in the detail it provides.

Being the only book on the Irish in Europe that was attempted in his lifetime, Davis's *Souvenirs* is a noteworthy, if imbalanced, scholarly effort. As its conclusion demonstrates, it was written with a particular purpose. By showing how Irish people had been able to 'reach the highest rungs of the social ladder and could rule and govern abroad', Davis sought to 'prove the absurdity' of the idea that they were incapable of governing themselves. The question of what sort of national government the Irish people might actually desire to see established is one which he does not answer. His failure to answer this question while attempting to 'prove' the reality of Irish nationality in a European context could be said to be of significance however. Notwithstanding his own belief that 'the spirit of modern progress' was in favour of democratic republics, Davis can generally think of no way of asserting Ireland's right to a place among the nations of Europe except by pointing to the power of Catholic Ireland during the early modern period, and by celebrating Ireland's Gaelic linguistic heritage; the latter being a quite unusual attitude to be held by a man of his generation. As such, it is not very surprising that once an independence movement arose in Ireland shortly after his death, it was primarily the 'Irish-Irelander' ideal and a pride in Ireland's Catholic heritage, rather than a democratic-republican radicalism, that captured the imagination of the public and, in turn, essentially gave the young Irish state its sense of identity, not only as a 'nation' but also in terms of being part of a greater European family.

APPENDIX: THE MUSE'S HOUR: A SELECTION OF DAVIS'S POETRY WRITTEN ON THE CONTINENT

Davis's verse has never appeared in compendiums of works by Irish poets. He himself prefaced the sole published volume of his verse with the dismissive remark that its contents were written merely 'in the rare intervals of leisure snatched from a pressman's busy life'. As 'Owen Roe' was generally best known during his lifetime as a poet rather than as a journalist, however, to complement the main text and to give an overall picture of his literary style, it has been decided to include ten of his poems here as an appendix. Like the main text, all were written during his 'sojourn on the continent' during the mid-1880s, with the exception of 'Lough Ine'. This appeared in the *Shamrock* during November 1877 and is perhaps the best example of his writing verse in a classic, romantic vein. The remainder have been selected from *A Vision of Ireland and other Poems* (Dublin, 1889). The humorous 'Count Camille's Bride' and the fiery 'Song of the Veteran Republican' are good examples of his fondness for continental-style melodrama, whereas the romantic piece 'Pisa' and the curiously bitter 'Chateaux en Espagne' relate more directly to his European travels. 'The Muse's Hour', where he contemplates his ambitions and failings both as a man and as a poet, is perhaps the most autobiographical of all his poems, while 'To K. M. M.' is one of the more interesting or least sentimental examples of his love poetry. 'The Admiral Villaret' is one of the best of the countless number of historical ballads he wrote during his career, while 'Orange and Green' was the most well known of all his nationalist lyrics. Finally, perhaps with a nod to Yeats, in 'An Irish Pagan Ode' he is seemingly drawing upon ancient Irish mythology for inspiration, portraying in dramatic terms the despair of 'the last of the Brehons' when deserted by their gods.

Souvenirs of Irish Footprints Over Europe

[. . .] in the text of *Souvenirs of Irish Footprints Over Europe* that follows indicates where the original text is not continuous in this edition. See pp. 9–10 above.

Chapter 1

Belgium

LOUVAIN

It was under a beautifully tinted autumnal sky that I caught the first glimpse of classic Louvain. Its dark medieval facades were aglow with prismatic colours; its winding streets were a confused mingling of light and shade; while the chimes or carillons, pealing from the towers, shed a subtle melody over the town. Louvain is situated in South Brabant and stands on the banks of the pleasant Dyle, some sixteen miles east of Brussels. It was for a long time the residence of the Dukes of Brabant and had in the Middle Ages flourishing woollen manufacturers which gave employment to 150,000 workmen. The weavers turned out to be a turbulent race – with the result that several thousands of them were expelled by the authorities and Louvain, like Antwerp, became a decaying centre. Its population is now only one-sixth of what it was several hundred years ago, and its present listless and dreary aspect contrasts singularly with the appearance it bore when the click of the loom was heard in every second house, and the democrats of those days would make periodical visits to the Town Hall and fling a baker's dozen of magistrates heels over heads out of the windows! Its only staple industry just now is somewhat of the Guinness type; 200,000 casks of beer are annually exported, and the quality of the liquid is considered excellent wherever it is quaffed outside the precincts of the town. In the town itself it is, however, execrable, the dregs of the brewery being exclusively reserved for the inhabitants. [. . .]

On the generally sound and wholesome principle that a man should always prefer the wines or beers of the country in which he travels to any foreign imports – granting, of course, that he be not afflicted with the virus of teetotalism – I made all conscientious efforts to patronise this white but slightly yellowish liquid. I sipped it in this 'brasserie' and in that, and even proceeded to headquarters and quaffed a glass thereof to the health of the director of the establishment, making wry faces all the while, much to the disgust of the obliging functionary; but I could not relish its insipidity. It looks at a distance like absinthe diluted with water; but it has not the dangerously inspiring fire or stamina of the French or Swiss commodity. To any thirsty visitor who may find himself perspiring on a sultry day in the streets of Louvain I would recommend a foaming glass of 'faro', a Brussels beer, which in colour is not so blonde as Bass, and yet not quite so brune as Guinness. The spring in the oasis may be very well in its way, but it cannot compare with the 'faro' when quaffed by one who is agonisingly in want of a drink. [. . .]

The old Irish College of Louvain is now, and has been for many years, a Christian Brothers' institution. It is a plain, unpretentious three-storeyed edifice; but the sombre air of antiquity that hovers around it has peculiar charms of its own for the student and the traveller. This historic pile stands at the corner of the Rue de Pantalu, to the rere of an enclosure which is separated from the street by a dingy and mouldering wall. This enclosure was in other days the 'cours d'honneur' of the college; but it is at the present moment a comparatively barren waste, relieved only by a few stunted trees that seem – particularly in the hoar winter time – to be so many gaunt weird spectres, keeping watch and ward over the solitude around. Over the door of the edifice one reads the inscription – 'Institut Saint Antoine, Dirige par les Freres de la Charite.'

When, in 1878, I visited the establishment for the first time, the courteous superior pointed me out in the hall entrance the slabs under which lie buried the mortal remains of Dr de Burgo, former Bishop of Elphin, and Rosa O'Doherty, the wife of Owen Roe O'Neill, and other sons and daughters of the old land. Owing to the fact that the slabs, situated, as they were on the floor, had been trodden by several generations, the inscriptions on the marble had become almost quite effaced. Shortly afterwards one of the Irish students of Louvain, the Rev. James Ryan, D.D., of the Archdiocese of Cashel, had the slabs taken up from under foot in the cloister passage and placed as mural adornments. Father Ryan was at the same time fortunate enough to secure the services of the Rev. Dr Ruyssens, Professor of Archaelogy in the University, who was enabled to procure correct copies of the effaced inscriptions. I may add here that the Rev. Father Cary, OSF., and Father O'Hanlon rendered Father Ryan all the necessary assistance in this laudable and patriotic undertaking of his. [. . .]

Dr Conry, the illustrious Archbishop of Tuam, who was a political refugee in Europe in those days, and whose remains are interred in St Anthony's cloisters, was the founder of the institution. The first practical step made by Dr Conry to supply the growing wants of Irish ecclesiastical students in Flanders was to petition the Spanish monarch, Philip III (who was then lord and master of the Lowlands) for the erection and endowment of a Franciscan convent in the city and University of Louvain. His Spanish Majesty immediately acceded to this request; for we find him on the 21st of September, 1606, signifying his pleasure to the Archduke Albert, Governor of the Low Countries, that Dr Conry's petition should be at once granted, and that one thousand Spanish ducats be allocated every year for the support of the college. [. . .] When the edifice was shortly afterwards completed, it was attached to the University by a special Bull of Pope Adrian VIII, its first president being Nicholas Aylmer, and one of its earliest students being the scholarly Nicholas French, who was subsequently consecrated Bishop of Ferns.

St Anthony's College soon became one of the chief schools on the Continent. Youths from all portions of Ireland came hither to pursue their ecclesiastical studies. Some remained in the land of their adoption to fill professorial chairs with the utmost credit to themselves, or to act the part of zealous missionaries in Switzerland and the Netherlands. Others – who formed, by the way, the considerable majority – returned to their native land in all manners of disguises in order to keep the lamp burning in the sanctuary, and lay down their lives, if necessary, for the Faith which they cherished, for the creed which had been banned and proscribed from sea to sea. [. . .]

The first guardian of St Anthony's was none other than Father Donatus Mooney, who, in a sense, may be called the founder of the Irish historical school established within the precincts of that institution. [. . .] He wrote in Latin the history of the Irish Franciscans, a work of much erudition, which has been in our own day embodied in Father Meehan's 'History of the Rise and Fall of the Irish Franciscan Monasteries.'

St Anthony's College will live chiefly in history as the institution where Brother O'Clery, the leading light of the Four Masters, matured that remarkable talent of his, and that untiring capacity for intellectual research, thanks to which we owe the 'Annals'. [. . .] It was in one of these little cells, chastily and severely furnished, that he often sat down to his table, and burned the midnight taper in careful study of the ancient Irish MSS which formed the glory and attraction of the library of the college in those days in the eyes of most of the scholars of Flanders. Brother O'Clery was a native of Donegal, and could traces his lineage to the brehons of the house of Tyrconnell. Learning was the traditional characteristic of his family, and well and faithfully did O'Clery adhere to the family tradition. Shortly after he conceived the idea of compiling the 'Annals', he left Louvain for Ireland in 1620, seven years before the flag of the Confederation waved from the towers of St Canice.[1] [. . .] When he had concluded his researches he retired with two scions of his own family and one of the O'Duigenans of Roscommon to the Friary of Donegal, that sanctuary of Irish lore, standing within touch of the billows, in solitude and seclusion, of which D'Arcy McGee so weirdly sings in his lines:

Whene'er I go, a pilgrim,
Back, dear holy isle, to thee,
May my filial footsteps bear me
To that abbey by the sea –
To that abbey, roofless, doorless,
Shrineless, monkless, though it be!

Some two hundred and fifty years ago it had its roof, its shrine, its portals and its monks. Here for a decade worked these four masters with the zeal and enthusiasm of the clerics of medieval monasteries, far from the clamour of the crowd and the giddy tumult of life, awaking each morn only to hear the swish of the waves on the desolate shore, and retiring to rest each eve with the same orchestral music pouring its lullabies into their ears. Even the cynic Bolingbroke,[2] who at one time pined, and pined in vain, for cloisters where the cult of learning should be exclusively carried out, might have found his beau ideal realised in this literary retreat away in distant Donegal. [. . .]

After having performed more than its part in supplying Ireland with priests throughout the Penal Days, St Anthony's College was, so to speak, swept away by the Revolution. In 1817, when the University of Louvain was re-established, the college was given over to the Christian Brothers, in whose possession it still is. The Irish students who pitched their tents on the banks of the Dyle since 1817 were attached to a purely Belgian institution, the Collège du Saint Esprit, the ecclesiastical department of the University. [. . .] It may not be out of place to mention here that in a later siege of Louvain, in 1830, when the Belgians were fighting gallantly for their national independence, a score or so of the Irish students of St Esprit doffed their soutanes for soldiers' uniforms, and defended one of the bridges on the Dyle successfully against the Dutch. The ten survivors of those brave young Irishmen subsequently received an enthusiastic ovation at the hands of the inhabitants, and were presented with golden medals, in compliment to their valour, at the conclusion of the campaign. [. . .]

The alumni of St Esprit enjoyed far more freedom than do the Levites of Maynooth or Carlow. They were not caged within stone walls ten months out of twelve. They were as free to stroll about the town outside class hours, whenever it pleased them to do so, as their colleagues of the law and medicine. They could even give entertainments in their rooms, sing songs, and utter extempore speeches, provided, of course, that they kept their mirth and joy within reasonable bounds. The genial professors who supervised the inner working of the college were general favourites, for they had always the knack of more than tempering justice with mercy, avoiding everything in the shape of stony rigidity, and pleased to see youth disporting itself innocently, after it had a victorious tussle with the profound syllogisms of Bouvier or the lighter lore of Gury.

One evening – I shall not for obvious reasons particularise the year or even the decade – one of the most respected prelates of the South of Ireland, since deceased, happened to steal a march on the young men from his diocese who were studying in Louvain. Having been informed by the porter of the number of the cell occupied by one of these gentlemen,[3] his lordship moved gently up the staircase, and was soon surprised to hear a decidedly un-Gregorian and jubilant song surging through the keyhole of the room which he intended to visit. He paused aghast for a few moments, and listened. 'Fill the Bumper Fair!' had just been completed, and 'God Save Ireland' was being intoned in spanking style. His lordship summoned up courage immediately and opened the door. Here, indeed, was a tableau for episcopal eyes to see! A half-filled bottle of John Jameson's whiskey, flanked by four glasses, and accompanied by the proper 'materials', stood on a table, around which sat four Irish students, enjoying themselves to their hearts' content!

When that right rev. prelate returned to Ireland his report had the effect of seriously diminishing the contingent of Irish students in Louvain. In 1878 they had dwindled down to five, representing respectively the dioceses of Ross, Cloyne, Ossory, Kerry and Down and Connor. In 1884 the last of Irish ecclesiastics ordained for Irish missions left Louvain for ever, bearing with him the green flag of the Hibernian alumni, emblazoned on one side by the arms of Leinster, Munster, Ulster and Connaught, and on the other by the arms of the University. This gentleman, who belonged to the diocese of Ossory, deposited the precious relic in St Kiernan's College, Kilkenny, where it remains on this day, a mute witness of the fact that Ireland proper no longer treads the cloister of Louvain. The only Irishmen at present residing in the town are those who are being educated in the American College, and who are destined for American missions. [. . .]

Louvain is, as your readers are aware, the seat of one of the oldest existing universities. It may be classified with those of Paris, Bologna, Padua and Salerno, and still remains a monument to the learning of those medieval times which the captious critics, or rather the sciolists of modern schools so flippantly regard as ignorant. It was founded in 1425 by a Bull of Pope Martin V, authorising the chapter of the cathedral of St Peter's to form classes for the education of the young. Shortly after its establishment it attained a

European reputation and scholars flocked to its halls from nearly every portion of the Continent – from the cities and towns amid the primeval forests of Germany, the vineyards of the Cid, the hill-sides and valleys of Greece, the recesses of Hungary, and the Lowlands. It was not till the 17th century that Irishmen frequented in large numbers this remarkable institution. A few of our countrymen studied within its precincts prior to that epoch, but records of them are very hard to find. [. . .]

Speculative philosophy formed the basis of the intellectual training of the alumni. Those were days, of course, when in the domain of abstract thought Plato's theories, leavened with the Christian spirit, ruled the roast; when Bacon's inductive method was still undreamt of, and when experimental investigations into the laws of bodies had not yet become the hobbies of master minds. The chief questions discussed in these halls at the time I refer to were themes that had a wondrous attraction for the public opinion of Europe, but which are now rarely, if ever, discussed outside the confines of ecclesiastical seminaries or monasteries. Entity and essence, the attributes of the Son of God, the damning point in the latest heresy or the most profound item in the latest dogma, were problems that convulsed learned Europe at that time, and formed materials for many a thesis in which the doctors of Padua would cross intellectual swords with the doctors of the Sorbonne, and objections to any given theory would be made in Louvain, to be awarded a ready and echoing answer from the active brain-machinery of Salerno. When the number of students in Louvain rose to 6,000, and the fame of its professors was contributing to render it the rendezvous of the talent of Europe, the big-wigs of the Sorbonne took umbrage at its growing proportions, and strained every nerve to outrival their colleagues on the banks of the Dyle. The contest between both learned corporations ultimately ended, however, in a drawn battle, although Paris could boast of having nurtured some of the most intensely speculative geniuses of the day, among them being the unfortunate Abelard,[4] whose Platonic propensities were nevertheless not strong enough to save him from the temptations of the 'sweet soft passion'.[5] [. . .]

The Louvain University pursued the tenour of its ways for almost four hundred years. The tenour was not, it must be added, an altogether even one; for this Arcadian retreat of learning was sometimes ruthlessly broken in upon by vandal enemies from without and restless spirits within. The turbulent weavers, to whom reference has been already made, had, I fear, but a scanty share of respect for the occupants of the University. In the estimation of the woollen manufacturers, students and professors were probably considered to be no better than idle dawdlers or the vainest of dreamers; for even then there was a certain incipient relish for utilitarianism in humanity. However that may have been, the handy-men of the loom and the votaries of learning sometimes dealt each other sound drubbings in the city streets. [. . .] On other occasions, the Dutch or some other foreign foe would cross the border and the students would abandon their musty tomes and gird on their swords, and stand by the side of the weavers, and gallantly defend the town against the invaders. They had not forgotten Horace's maxim, that it was sweet and honourable to die for one's country. Scholars were soldiers as well in those 'brave days of old'. And when the town was saved, or when peace was signed, those juveniles, or rather those of their number who survived, would dip once more into the pages of Cornelius a Lapide,[6] and turn from the tocsin of war to the inspiration of classic or scholastic lore.

A time was, however, coming when the labours of the students were to be suspended for almost a generation and the halls of the university were to be diverted from their original purposes. It was immediately after the epoch when the *Encyclopaedia* was startling the world with new but absurd and impossible theories; when

Voltaire was pouring the vials of his wrath on Christianity from his hermitage in Ferney; when Jean Jacques Rousseau was penning his *Confessions*, his *Nouvelle Heloise*, and his *Contrat Social* in Swiss chalets or in the faubourgs of Paris; and when Condorcet was sapiently discovering the advent of the much-talked-of millennium.[7] The teachings of these philosophers had their inevitable result in the Reign of Terror of 1793. The Revolution of 1789 was the legitimate revolt of a long-injured and outrageously oppressed people against unscrupulous and exacting taskmasters. The overthrow of the hated Bastille was the overthrow of an old world and the foundation of a new; but unfortunately the democratic movement of that day fell into the hands of sanguinary daredevils like Marat and Robespierre, and paved the way ultimately for the dictatorship of a Napoleon. In that awful cataclysm, Republicanism of the European school received a staggering blow, from which it has not by any means as yet recovered, and from which it is not likely to recover for some time to come.

It was in the midst of this revolutionary whirlwind that the French troops entered the town of Louvain, and by orders of their commander-in-chief, ratified by the Paris Directory, the time-honoured university was immediately suppressed. The professors were summarily dismissed and the students dispersed. And so ended for a time the career of this learned institution. The buildings of the University were converted into hospitals and barracks, and Louvain itself became a garrison town. When Napoleon's triumphs were over, and the Imperial captive, after his defeat at Waterloo, was imprisoned in St Helena, Louvain began to breathe freely once more. The inhabitants immediately inaugurated a popular movement for the restoration of the university. The old building still stood as formerly in the heart of the town, but its interior resembled that of a huge mausoleum. After several petitions to the Dutch government, its portals were once more opened in 1817 to the students, and professors were appointed to conduct the classes. It never, however, recovered its ancient prestige. The Revolution of 1830, which made Belgium an independent nation, lent some additional vigour to the institution, and shed a brighter glow over its collegiate halls; but their medieval splendour had gone for ever. Louvain, it must be added, is not the only university whose ancient laurels exist no longer. In fact, of all the universities of the Middle Ages, not one today holds intact its past prestige. Padua and the Sorbonne, Bologna and Salerno, are but shadows of their former selves. Still Louvain keeps up its old traditions very valiantly indeed. It now contains some seven or eight hundred students and seventy-five professors. Twenty of the forty-five colleges which were formerly attached to it still belong to the 'alma mater'. [. . .]

The Church of St Peter in this city, containing as it does the ashes and bust of Dr Thomas Stapleton, the only Irishman who filled the exalted position of Rector of the University, must be an object of interest to every Irish visitor. The edifice was founded in 1040, but having been twice burned, the existing building is not older than 1430.

The interior of St Peter's, like the interior of many other medieval churches, is weirdly but beautifully sombre. Its darkest recesses are somewhat relieved by the rich colourings of the paintings from Flemish masters that deck the walls; while the quaint old pillars that still defy the ravages of time, and the superb pulpit of massive oak, with its carved figures and its allegories starting, so to speak, vividly from the wood, impress the spectator with the idea that the architects of the past knew well how to plan edifices that might shelter a decade or so of generations and still look the storm as steadily in the face as ever.

We rear our stately piles nowadays with something approaching electric speed; we trick them out in meretricious finery, and admire them with snug complacency, crying out the while, with Keats, that a thing of beauty is a joy for ever. Yet if we could only see a few inches beyond our noses we might discover that our gilded architectural creations are like the apples gathered on the Dead Sea shore – consumptive at heart and doomed to immediate decay. Thoughts such as these often occurred to me while I gazed on the façade of Notre Dame in Paris or sauntered through the glorious isles of San Pietro in Rome. Here in St Peter's of Louvain, too, the traveller has occasion to reflect on the fact that the architects who planned the edifice, the deft as well as sinewy hands that built it, and the sculptors and painters whose genius embellished it with such lasting grandeur, must have passed away for ever without leaving any heirs of their name or fame behind.

Dr Stapleton, whose remains are interred in this church, was a native of the county Tipperary, having been born in the little town of Fethard. Early in life he found that no opportunities were afforded him of acquiring suitable education in his native land. He accordingly proceeded to Louvain, where, after a brilliant curriculum, he bore off the degree of Doctor of Canon Law, and was shortly afterwards nominated to the position of president of the College of Mechlin. He was subsequently promoted from this post to the more exalted one of 'Rector Magnificus' of the University of Louvain, and became at the same time one of the canons attached to St Peter's. While attending to the responsible duties of both these offices Dr Stapleton found time to take an active and patriotic interest in the administration of St Anthony's Irish College in the town; for it was under his auspices that the first complete fount of Gaelic type that ever existed was manufactured in that establishment. There was, however, a Gaelic fount working there shortly before Dr Stapleton became rector, a fount that produced such works as the 'Irish Catechism' of Dr Conry; Dr Hugh MacCaghwell's 'Mirror of Penance', published in 1618; the 'Glossary', written by the illustrious annalist, Michael O'Clery, in 1643, and other volumes from the pens of such distinguished Irish hagiologists as Colgan, Gernon, and MacGillacuddy. In a manuscript catalogue of the books that issued from the Irish College of Louvain, and bearing the date of 1675, I find the following allusion to this Gaelic fount:

> In a plain chest is preserved the type of the printing press; the key is over the chest. In the pulpit there is one silver chalice belonging to the convent of Donegal, a small case of the relics of various saints, and the silver seal belonging to O'Donnell. In the first of the upper rooms in a small chest is the Irish type with its own forms; also several copies of Colgan's works, Ward's 'St Rumold', the 'Fochloir' (O'Clery's Glossary) and some skins for the cover of books.

From the 'History of the Franciscan Order', published in 1630, we learn that 'the Irish convent of Louvain, for the salvation of souls in the kingdom of Ireland, had established in the year 1611 a printing press with the proper type for the Irish letters, which, on account of the prevailing heretical rule, was heretofore impracticable to the Catholics of that kingdom, and printed some books in the Irish language, to the great advantage of the faithful.' It may be added here that Father Hussey composed in Louvain a metrical Irish catechism in two hundred and forty verses, which a century later was published by Donlevy as an appendix to the latter's famous catechism in the same tongue. There are other poems by the same rev. writer which are still preserved in the archives of the Royal Irish Academy in Dublin.

Dr Stapleton completed the Gaelic fount referred to, and published through its medium an 'Irish Grammar for Students', which soon became a class-book not only in Louvain but also in several other Continental universities. [. . .]

To the left of the high altar in St Peter's one can see the Stapleton Memorial. In a niche stands the bust of the illustrious Irish scholar, representing him in his declining years, after he had won all the intellectual laurels he ambitioned. The features are rather rough and rugged; but the high grappling brow is deeply impressive, and the head is of purely classic mould. At the right of the bust stands a statuette of Science, in the shape of a young maiden with bowed head and dishevelled locks, holding in one of her hands a broken lamp. To the left one sees a statuette of Fate, with a grinning skull in his fleshless palm. Overhead is the ghastly figure of Death wielding his traditional scythe. There is a Latin inscription on a tablet which is attached to the wall immediately underneath the bust. [. . .]

Among the more eminent of the lay professors of Louvain who held chairs in the university immediately prior to its suppression by the French revolutionists, I find one who bears the suspiciously Irish nomenclature of O'Halloran. An adventurous Hibernian this same O'Halloran must have been, if we are to trust the testimony of an old Louvain archaeologist, who told me wondrous things about him. Like Bagenal in his day,[8] and O'Shea in ours,[9] O'Halloran scoured Europe from end to end with a pilgrim's knapsack on his back. It is said that he used to boast with pride in the library of Louvain University that he had trodden more square feet of the continent than any man either living or dead! True, he did not push the programme of his explorations beyond the confines of Europe. In regard to extent of travel, he could not, I admit, hold a farthing candle to Buck Whalley, who for a bet made in Daly's Club in Dublin did actually play ball against the walls of Jerusalem; but O'Halloran knew Europe as well as a scrupulous and scholarly Low Churchman knows the Thirty-nine Articles. He had palmed himself off in Madrid as a full-blown 'caballero', with his features dyed to the proper sallow height of tint, and the proportions of his muscular frame displayed to the best advantage under the folds of the inevitable mantilla. In that beautiful land of olive groves and garlic O'Halloran disported himself with all the ease of the gayest of butterflies. His suave manners, his oily tongue, and his herculean build must have told on the romantic hearts of the languishing senoritas of the South, with some of whom this Irish knight-errant used to hold innocent flirtations – just to pass the golden hours away when the clamour or excitement of the Puerta del Sol would pall on his sight.

We discover him subsequently twisting his tongue around the guttural German in a little village on the banks of the Rhine; paying his respects throughout the summer at the shrine of 'bock-beer' in Munich, wearing a turban and sporting a fez on the banks of the Bosphorus, where he studied the Khoran; and though a Christian, accomplished the hitherto unparalleled feat of entering a mosque, shoeless and prayerful, in the disguise of a Mussulman![10] If the Grand Vizier had only the faintest idea of such a sacrilegious escapade on the part of O'Halloran that worthy would never have become professor in the University of Louvain; for he would, if caught in the act, have been flayed alive, and his body would have been artistically carved by dutiful knives in order to appease the anger of the mighty Allah.

O'Halloran, having been eventually suspected of instigating a rebellion against the Sultan, had to fly from the imperial police, and proceeded to Russia, where he lived, wrapped up in luxurious furs, till he got lost one bleak evening in the snows of Siberia; and, after a merciless winter spent in that solitude in attempts to regain the haunts of civilisation, he at least found means to steer his course to Norway and Sweden. It is recorded of him that in his travels through these new countries as well as in his travels through France and Italy he hardly ever entered a post-chaise. Today, the biggest boor going – if he have but a plethoric purse – can cover in a very short time two-thirds of the habitable globe, lolling on a dainty cushion, and dissecting men and things from the window of a railway compartment, and come home with a three-volume dissertation on his experiences abroad. Such a fellow knows as little of the habits and customs of the people he has seen as I do of the South Sea Islanders. O'Halloran, however, was living at a time when the steam engine was still undreamt of. He scorned to have recourse to the free-and-easy conveyances of his day – even when he had to cross the Alps, trudge up and down the Apennines or bivouac on the heights of the Pyrenees. He tramped on foot with jaunty step all over the Continent.

He had sown the last of his wild oats before he returned to Louvain. On reaching that town his unquestionable talents were recognised by the directing committee of the University, who offered him the chair of European literature in the college of the Holy Trinity in that town. O'Halloran was pre-eminently well fitted for such a position. He was proficient in at least eight European languages. He wrote verses equally well in English and Irish, and could turn a sonnet in the sweet Tuscan tongue with as much bewitching finesse as if he were born and reared within sight of the Duomo of Florence and had spent his nights over the poems of Petrarch. We have the authority of Father Victor de Buck, the distinguished Bollandist,[11] for the statement that O'Halloran penned remarkably credible Flemish verses – a feat that no foreigners to Flanders ever accomplished or ever will accomplish.

Like all great scholars, the professor had his weak points. Nature with a sly malice of her own loves to create imperfections – at least in flesh in blood – to remind us, I fancy, as Philip's slave used to remind his master, that we are but mere mortals after all. Nature gave Byron a fine intellect; but she took care to dilute the wine with water by cursing him with a lame leg. Professor O'Halloran's foible was an overweening vanity – a foible, by the way, common to most people who find themselves well provided for physically and intellectually. He had a splendid physique, to be admired by pit and gallery, and sound and brilliant talents to catch the fancy of even the most dyspeptic critics in the Press box. [. . .] Like the celebrated German barber, O'Halloran came to the conclusion that the only three great men whom the eighteenth century produced were himself, Voltaire, and the King of Prussia! The poor Professor, however, with all his high notions, cannot say with the Roman bard: '*Non omnis moriar*.'[12] Despite all his talents and accomplishments he is now almost as much forgotten as if he never lived. He has left no learned tomes after him to create a school or keep his name before the public; and although I spent many a weary hour in the University library with my archaeological friend, hunting up every possible record in which I may have alighted on topography of his grave, I failed piteously in the attempt. Like the wild flowers of the forest, he shed his fragrance on the air for a little while and then melted like its aroma into empty space![13]

Peradventure, the only Irish historical importance that can be attached to the personality or career of O'Halloran is the fact that he was at one time a professor of Daniel O'Connell. It is not generally known that the great Irish Tribune, before going to St Omer's, studied for a year or two in the College of the Holy Trinity of Louvain – an establishment which still exists as the Collège des Josephites, and which would well merit the attention of a visit at the hands of the Irish tourist in Belgium. The Holy Trinity College in the last century was chiefly the haunt of juveniles of wealthy and aristocratic houses. Its alumni were, however, of very tender years, for it was only a preparatory school at the best of times. It was here where the scion of Derrynane first learned the French language, in which, we are told, he was such an adept throughout his subsequent career.

An officious cicerone pointed me out what he called O'Connell's autograph on one of the doors of this institution; but, unlike the Jew Appela, I felt myself conscientiously bound to be incredulous. The autograph was evidently written with a large bodkin in a Vere Foster schoolboy hand; but it had a suspiciously modern look about it that crushed every temptation I may have had to subscribe with beating heart to its authenticity.

A waggish guide tried to play on me the scurvy trick of passing off a scrawl on the wall of a tumble-down rookery in Genoa as the autograph of Christopher Columbus. When I visited Verona a short time ago I was almost wheedled into the belief that a 'William Shakespeare', which I had seen scribbled over the so-called tomb of fair Juliet in that town, was in the great dramatist's handwriting, till on reflection I discovered that that illustrious Britisher had never set foot in Italy. I found out shortly afterwards that the autograph was penned by one of the ever-increasing troop of British tourists who affect the southern peninsula – one of those trumpery Shakespeares who visited the place in the fifties of the present century, and who on the strength of having the same name as the immortal William, audaciously hoodwinked the simple-minded Veronese into the idea that he was a lineal descendant of the Bard of Avon! I must not, however, in all justice, make the sweeping declaration that all the autographs one sees abroad are not authentic. Every man of the English, American, and, I fear I must add, Irish, tourist type is not satisfied with himself while in Rome until he has profanely carved the outlines of his obscure name on the broken pillars of the Forum or on the walls of the Colosseum. I saw a few score of such nomenclatures, 'born, perhaps, to blush unseen', but still blushing very visibly indeed from the leaning tower of Pisa; I have seen the same very questionable calligraphic ornaments in the interior of the turrets of Notre Dame, and beheld them even elbowing their impudent way to the pillars of the Arc du Triomphe, cheek-by-jowl with the names of the illustrious generals of the First Empire! What information posterity will glean from the autographs of these globe-trotters Heaven only knows! I might say here that the only authentic autograph of a great man on stone walls abroad, before which one can bow down in simple faith and sincere admiration, is that of Lord Byron on Bonivard's pillar in Chillon, carved as it is in the fine large Roman hand of the wandering Childe Harold. When I saw it in the springtide of 1886, as I was exploring the beauties of Lake Leman, I had made sufficient inquiry, circumstantial and otherwise, to warrant me in upholding its authenticity.

There are no autographs of Oliver Goldsmith on post or pillar in Louvain, although the bard was, we are told, at one time a resident of the city, where he earned his bread by piping on his flute in the streets, or teaching English in return for French in the chambers of the students. It is also on record that the eccentric but good-natured Irish troubadour used to attend classes in the University and enjoyed quite a peculiar delight in the study of botany. Louvain cannot take to itself the credit of having awarded a degree to the genius who was considered a blockhead by the white-kidded gentry of Trinity. Heidelberg University honoured 'Noll' with the title by which Johnson in subsequent years almost invariably addressed him. The house in Louvain in the top garret of which Goldsmith vegetated for a few months has been long since demolished; but the Town Hall, which the poet so admired, is still as bewilderingly beautiful as it was in his day, with its exquisitely sculptured facades and its stately walls, in which there are hundreds of niches where the statues of the scholars and warriors of Flanders, dust-worn but majestic, look down from the far past, as it were, on the pigmies of today, who have replaced the giants of yesterday in the square below.

Mark O'Sullivan, who hailed from the Kingdom of Kerry, was, I believe, the last Irish lay student who walked the corridors of the University of Louvain where he enjoyed a 'bourse d'etudes' founded in that city during the penal days by one of his ancestors. When I met O'Sullivan for the first time, in 1878, he had been for fourteen years a resident of Louvain. His name figured on the University roll, and I verily believe he used to attend lectures once in a while, say with every new moon; but I quite forget just now what particular kind of diploma he was in quest of. He may have ambitioned becoming a big-wig of the schools, a barrister at the Brussels Bar, a luminary in the

Belgian medical firmament, or a possible rival of De Lesseps in the engineering department. In any case, he had determined to live and die on Belgian soil. He had become so much acclimatised to the land of his adoption, and had mixed so much with its inhabitants, that he was more Belgian than the Belgians themselves. Yet, withal, although he spoke English with a decidedly foreign accent, his tongue in wagging never lost in peculiar Irish witchery and he kept up his acquaintance with the Gaelic authors to the end. One day, while he was attending the Literature and Language class in the University, the Professor and Mark had quite an interesting passage-at-arms. The Professor, who was a most accomplished linguist and a disci-pline and admirer of the great Mezzophanti, determined on testing the knowledge of his pupils in the various tongues. None were found competent to discuss any subject with the learned man in more than three languages – Latin, French and Flemish – until it came to the turn of the Irishman, who, to the utter bewilderment of his colleagues, kept up a running fire with the Professor not merely in Latin, French and Flemish, but in Greek, Italian, Spanish, and German as well; and eventually, when Mark put a poser to his antagonist in Irish, and the latter failed to reply, a cheer rang from the lips of the assembled students, and O'Sullivan was dubbed by universal acclaim as the Irish Polyglot of Louvain.

Mark and I used sometimes to saunter out of the town in the mellow autumn evenings to a pretty little rustic café in the environs, where, seated on the terrace outside, we would discuss philology and faro beer till the twilight shadows warned us off. Mark was, like the wonderful Professor Mortimer Murphy of Paris, a 'peripatetic encyclopaedia of information'. His mind was, if I may so speak, a well-stocked granary of facts and dates; and yet his conversation was not that of a pedant or a dry-as-dust archaeologist, for he used to garnish every theme he discussed with the spicy attic sauce of wit and humour, expressed in the mellifluous accents of his Kerry brogue. He was a confirmed sceptic, however, on most points. Although not much over thirty years of age at the time, he had outgrown nearly all his enthusiasm, and looked on the world as a stage and on life as a comedy. The only subject that evoked anything approaching passionate ardour on his part was the proud record of the family of which he was a member. 'I am the son of a kingly stock', he would say, 'and, despite all the democratic drivelling of the age, I hold that blue blood has more sterling honour in its current than red!' Max O'Rell, an irrepressible literary wag, it was who said that he never yet met an Irishman who did not boast of being a lineal descendant of one of the monarchs of ancient Erin. 'Those monarchs of ancient Erin must have been *grands gallards* in their day', added the witty writer, 'for they evidently practised Mormonism before the coming of the Mormons!' O'Sullivan would scorn to acknowledge himself as a mere scion of the Princes of Beare. He would go back for his ancestry a thousand and odd years before the building of the Castle of Dunboy, till his fancy would be lit up with radiant visions of the Ard Righ, his Ollamhes and Brehons, his bards and pages standing on the field of a cloth of gold, and dispensing justice to a grateful and contented people.

Mark, or, as he would classically put it, Marcus, was a Royalist, and would have no objection to don the purple of his ancestors – if the purple and the throne were to be had for the asking. Sometimes a group of gay, rollicking students would invade the café, and sing lively ditties over their cups. War, wine and women – that inseparable trio – formed the burden of almost every chorus. Republican lyrics were generally tabooed by the Louvain students; but when a few strays and waifs from the Brussels University came down off and on to these monarchical regions, the 'Marseillaise' would burst gloriously from their parted lips, to the inexpressible anguish of Mark, who once confessed to me that though the 'Boyne Water' was bad enough, Rouget de Lisle's piece of lyrical buffoonery was infinitely worse!

One evening in particular we found ourselves much interested in the antics of a Cockney tourist, dressed in orthodox tweed, and gazing on all the surroundings with the air and attitude of one who has just dropped from a higher sphere. The afternoon was more than usually sultry and our tourist was evidently a thirsty soul. 'I say, guv'nor', exclaimed the Britisher, 'have you got any gingerbeer?' The proprietor of the café grinned and looked into vacancy. 'I say, guv'nor', cried the exasperated tweed-suited visitor, 'get me ginger-beer, or soda-water or lemonade, or lime juice, or anything in that line, you know.' The governor jabbered a reply in Flemish to the effect that English was not spoken on his premises, whereupon the Britisher rose in high dudgeon, calling him a stupid loon, and shrieked for a cup of tea. The landlord understood, or thought he understood, and soon afterwards came out with a bowl of transparent liquid called 'tisane', made from a decoction of herbs and said to be as much a cure for all ills on the continent as whiskey is supposed to be in certain quarters of Ireland. What a wry face that Cockney assumed while sipping the strange beverage! And how he reviled the stupidity of those foreigners who had nothing better to give a fellow to drink! And yet this pompous prig did not understand that he was for the time being in a country where the Blue Ribbon Army is quite an unknown factor, where, considered in a certain sense, teetotalism is scouted as the craze of fanatics, and where, nevertheless, drunkenness is by no means as rife as it is in the slums of London or the purlieus of Manchester. There are some people who judge foreign habits and customs from their own peculiar standpoint. A bullfight in Madrid is condemned by delicately reared gentry, who go with light hearts pigeon-shooting around the manors of Kent. Folk are altogether too fond of looking on themselves as paragons of perfection and thanking God with the Pharisee, that they are not as others! Virtue elbows vice and vice elbows virtue in every country under the sun. No nation in this respect can lay claim to the palm of any self-sufficient superiority.

O'Sullivan and I made many pilgrimages to places of interest in and around Louvain. One of these was the historic Mont Caesar, or 'Castrum Ceasaris', as it is called in the scholastic annals of the town. A gloomy, venerable, and yet romantic pile is this castle of the great Roman. Popular tradition has it that the edifice was built by Julius of that name during his sojourn among 'the bravest of the Gauls'. Here Charles, Archduke of Austria, the son of Philip and Joanna of Castille, known in history as Charles the Fifth, spent his dreamy youth, working out ambitious designs; and here he came in subsequent years, after he had worn a jewelled crown, attired in the humble habit of a monk weary of the cares of life and sick of the world's vanities. Here, too, was the residence of the poet and historian, Puteanus,[14] the worthy discipline of the scholarly Justin Lipsis.[15] Within these sombre bastions wended the footsteps of Hugh O'Neill and his fellow-exiles in 1607, when they took up their temporary residence in Louvain, where they received a warm ovation at the hands of the sturdy Flemish burghers. Tyrconnel and his friends lived, we are told, in the city; but by the express wish of the Archduke Albert, Hugh O'Neill had his home in the old Castle of Caesar. It was here the illustrious Irishman received deputations from the Irish students of the University and letters of sympathy and congratulation from the Irish prelates and scholars of Paris, Rome, and Douai. [. . .] There are other Irish associations, equally interesting, connected with this castle. It was at one of its gates, which is now little better than a ruin, that Preston and his Irish troops camped for several nights during the memorable siege of Louvain.[16] [. . .] A few yards distant, situated between the rocky stairs and the road which leads to the canal, stood the old Irish Dominican Convent, some of the cloisters of which establishment still survive the ravages of time. Historians state that it was Richard Bermingham, of the convent of Athenry, who procured for the Irish Dominicans their house of Mont Caesar. Its first rector was Oliver Burke, a native of Galway.

The site of the institution is now almost altogether occupied by private houses of comparatively modern growth. Before taking possession of the convent near the castle the Irish Dominicans had their residence in the Rue St Jacques. When they left Mont Caesar they opened a convent in a street in Louvain, which is called to this day 'la Rue des Dominicains Irlandais'. [. . .]

Various pilgrimages were also made to the site once occupied by the Irish Pastoral College of Louvain – an institution which must not be confounded with St Anthony's. This establishment was founded in 1625 and had for its object the education of Irish secular ecclesiastics destined for the Irish Mission. The pathway through life of many of these devoted men lay from Louvain to Ireland and from Ireland to the Tower of London, where the block and axe lay in wait for their summary execution. O'Sullivan called this college 'a nursery of martyrs', and he was literally as well as figuratively correct in his definition. The College itself, with its colossal archway spanned by the inscription, 'Collegium Hibernorum', has long since disappeared, and where it stood in the Rue des Orphelins one now beholds a children's hospital. It may be of interest to note that when the venerable building was vacated by the Irish in 1773, the Freemasons of Louvain became its owners and held their first banquet in its quaint old chapel. The building fell into ruin in the beginning of this century and was never restored. [. . .]

Our last pilgrimage was to Montaigu, a village situated a few miles north-east of Louvain. Here sleep a large number of Irish dead – soldiers and ecclesiastics, whose remains lie in unknown graves. There is, however, in this quaint old cemetery a large slab erected to the memory of Dr John O'Sullivan, of Kerry, who was Professor of Theology in the Irish Pastoral College, and one of the most distinguished scholars of Flanders in the last century. The inscription on the slab is now completely effaced, but I learned on excellent authority that the ecclesiastic whose memory it honours was born in the townland of Cappacusheen, in the barony of Dunkerron, within the shadow of Mangerton. I have been told – but I cannot vouch for the accuracy of the statement – that a roughly-hewn stone still marks the site of the house in which he first saw the light – lying at a side of the old road that extends from Sneem to Kenmare. O'Sullivan left the 'Kingdom' at an early age, and having prosecuted his studies with much success in the University, he was very soon afterwards promoted to a professor's chair. Montaigu, where his grave can still be seen, is at present a favourite resort of pilgrims.

It was after this visit to the home of Ireland's dead that I saw Mark O'Sullivan for the last time; for early next day I proceeded to Mechlin, and from thence to Brussels. A year or so subsequently an Irish friend in Namur wrote to me to Paris informing me that the Hibernian Polyglot was no more. Peace to the ashes of this brilliant though erratic genius!

BRUSSELS, WATERLOO AND LANDEN

I had my first idea of Brussels from the lips of an hotel proprietor who told me in unctuous accents that it was a 'petit' Paris. As I had at the time only a very rudimentary notion of the French capital – a city which I had yet to visit – I failed to appreciate mine host's observation at its proper value. Since then, however, I have become wiser, and can therefore in all justice subscribe to its truth. Brussels is indeed a miniature of the big town on the banks of the Seine, and is in social life a pocket edition of that ponderous volume, the pages of which extend from Montmartre to the Quartier Latin. I confess I do not like these miniatures. Imitation, they say, is the best kind of flattery. Well, the Parisians ought to have a superlatively high opinion of themselves if they turn their gaze on Brussels, doing its level best to copy the Boulevards and the Bois de Boulogne. There is, candidly, too much of the ape in the imitative mania of these people to command anything like respect or admiration. Although Brussels is the capital of an independent nation, it takes its social code from the foreigner. There is an absence of what I may call the spirit of nationality in its citizens. True enough, they would fight to the death for their liberty if Frank or Teuton crossed the border; they take pride in their ancient Flemish language and still uphold some of the quaint customs and habits of their forefathers. But how happens it that snobocracy[17] wields such fatal influence over the burgesses? I have known genteel as well as shabby-genteel circles in Brussels where the Flemish tongue was considered as vulgar a mode of expression as Irish would be in the drawingroom of a Dublin West Britisher. High-born dames, daintily unpatriotic, flock to Paris off and on to consult Woerth, the sovereign man-milliner of the Rue de la Paix, on the latest cut of a ball-dress, or the shape of the newest corset. Parisian art fashions the fans of Brussels, gilding them with the etchings of Naiads and Hemydryads, Bacchants and Graces, modelled from the tiny faces and still tinier figures of the hoydens of St Cloud. Cambric handkerchiefs and pretty foulards are all Parisian importations. The beautifully small feet of the dames and damsels of fashion are encased in Parisian leather, wrought into exquisite shapes by the hands of Parisian bootmakers. I verily believe that there may be found here and there throughout the city certain noble ladies who send to Paris for their lace, although Brussels lace – next, of course, to the Irish – is considered to be the best and prettiest in Europe. And when these ladies retire to the privacy of their chambers and dive into the mysteries of the toilette-table, the rouge which they coyly apply to their lips and the rice-powder with which they ruthlessly besmear their lovely countenances are fabricated within a stone's throw of the Seine. Articles having the Parisian brand upon them are in most cases preferred to the native creations –

it is so very, very fashionable and such good form, you know, to share the delicacies partaken of by the dainty duchesses and dowager duchesses of the great Faubourg St Germain!

As for the uglier portion of humanity in Brussels, it naturally takes its cue from the fairer. The dudes of the Belgian capital are imitation jewels of the genuine commodity on the boulevards. The Brussels shopkeeper is a second edition of his Parisian colleague – a little smuttier perhaps in appearance and a little less polite in his language and habits, but still the resemblance between both is too striking to be ignored. French politics, moreover, have more interest for the Brussels folk than their own. They will read with bated breath reports of the proceedings in the French Chamber of Deputies and yawn lazily over the harangues one hears in their own dull, stolid parliament at home. There is one feature in their imitative art that has, strange to say, been hitherto to a great extent neglected. They have not as yet created a spurious Belgian Boulanger – the inevitable hero with the blue sparkling Celtic eyes, the blonde beard, the richly caparisoned black steed and the other equally interesting accessories that frame in the tableau of the coming ruler of France.[18] I would not be astonished to hear any of these mornings that a brand new Boulanger has started to life on the asphalt of the capital of Flanders.

Brussels can never be a happy hunting-ground for tramcar shareholders, laid out as it is on hills and in valleys like a village in the Oberland. It is divided into the upper and lower towns, in the former of which the tinselled aristocracy loll their lazy lives away, the abyss at their feet being relegated to the multitude, washed and unwashed. In the fashionable quarter stands the King's Palace, where poor, inoffensive Leopold seeks shelter, as Louis of Versailles did in his forge, to screen himself from the feuds and bickerings of party cliques. Here also we find the Parliament House and the park, within which was once situated the old chateau of the brave Dukes of Brabant. The Palais de Justice, or, in other words, the Brussels Four Courts, [. . .]

is considered a beautiful building by others than Cook's tourists; while the Theatre Royal and the New Exchange might well merit a similar compliment. Irish visitors to Brussels will, however, take more interest in sauntering into the Place Royale, where stands, to the right of St James's Church, the King's Library. In this building there are veritable treasures of Irish archaeological lore. [. . .]

The Brussels Royal Library is one of the most valuable of its kind in Europe. It is peculiarly rich in old MSS in the Latin, Greek, Flemish, Irish, French, and Spanish languages. The building itself is separated from the street by a courtyard, at the outer door of which stand two of King Leopold's sentinels. Entering by the inner portal the visitor mounts a stone staircase, and on arriving at the second landing he discovers, to his left, a door over which is written 'Section des Bourgignons', or the Burgundy section – a part of the library exclusively devoted to manuscript literature. Having had a note of introduction to the amiable and learned librarian, M. Reubens, I was afforded by that gentleman every facility in exploring the purely Irish department. 'There are still some of your countrymen', he said, 'who cannot visit Brussels without coming to see the Burgundy collection; but they are very few.' The large room, in which I found myself, had nothing abnormal in its aspect. Budding historians, and historians who may have already blossomed; antiquated antiquaries and elderly spinsters of the blue-stocking texture pored through their spectacles over the dusty tomes of past centuries at the various tables, trying to decipher characters that looked suspiciously like hieroglyphics and taking copious notes of the contents. One of the group to whom I was presented by Monsieur Reubens, a venerable professor from one of the German universities, was in a veritable ecstasy as I entered. He had discovered some new theory on the origin of the cockle shells which were found on the summit of the Apennines. 'I now know how they got there', exclaimed the Teuton, in a paroxysm of joy, 'and *mehercule*! I will give the world a book that shall confound Voltaire in his version of the story.' I have seen some young and beardless bards when they read for the first time their productions in all the glory of print; I have seen more than one author hug his first book to his bosom as a father would his babe; I have seen the light in the child's eyes when toy soldiers in buskin and cakes of sugar-candy are poured liberally into his lap; but I never witnessed such an expansion of delight on any of these countenances that could compare with the aureole that had settled down on the parchment face of this happy professor. Despite the rheumatics attendant on old age, he actually pirouetted around the room like a dancing Dervish. Had he not made a grand discovery, and would not his name, as some poetaster put it, go ringing down sempiternally through the corridors of fame? The professor's revelations, I must judiciously add, are not yet in the publisher's hands, nor, I fancy, are they likely to be.

The MSS of the Irish part of this section are in Latin and Gaelic, the oldest of which date so far back as 1410. Some of the folios treat of St Brendan, the founder of the See of Ardfert, and enter into exhaustive details of the man who is reputed to have set foot on American soil before Christopher Columbus. I find in the same collection learned essays by Thomas Fleming, entitled 'De Rebus Hibernicis', written in 1612; poems in Latin on the state of Ireland, in a bulky quarto volume; Lives of Irish Saints, by Brother Clery; a list of the Franciscan Provincial monks who refused to adopt the tenets of Lutheranism, among them being Dermot O'Fogarty, Donald O'Cuenan and Dermot McEgan O'Donocha. Much time and labour were expended on the latter folio, a note in the last page of which informs us that it was finished in the Friary of Donegal on the 7th day of August 1613. Next in order is a poem in Gaelic, entitled 'Slios Daill Gulban McNeill' (1642), followed by Clery's Wars of the Irish and the Danes, a translation of which into English has been published from the pen of Dr Todd and may be found in the Master of the Rolls series in the reading-room of the Royal Irish Academy. This MS, which contains a very graphic account of the battle of Clontarf, was written in Donegal, and concluded there in November, 1635. I happened on a letter penned on a fly-leaf of this folio by Eugene O'Curry calling into question the authorship of a certain Gaelic poem, and dated 'Dublin, October, 1853'. One of the most interesting curiosities in the series is a Latin volume, 'Liber Purcelli et Monei', a comprehensive history of the Franciscan Order in Order in Ireland by Fathers Purcell and Mooney, a beautiful English version of which we owe to the talented pen of Father C. P. Meehan. On the flyleaf of this MS I read that Brother Anthony Purcell collected most of the materials for it by the express order of Provincial Brother Donat Mooney.

Another large folio embraces a Life of St Patrick and a copy of his 'Purgatorium', a French MS translation of which, illustrated by an Irish monk, holds a high place of honour in the Burgundian section. In addition to these we have the obituary of the monks of St Anthony's of Louvain, where we find such names as Blake, Fleming, de Burgo, Eugene McCarthy, Peter Morphy, and Patrick O'Connor, the last of whom is referred to as a lay brother and 'arte sartor'. Next in order are the lives of St Brigid and St Brendan of Clonfert, in Irish; a duodecimo volume containing the martyrology of Ireland's saints, by Brother Clery, and characterised by all that ecclesiastic's careful penmanship and exquisite formation of letters; a discussion on some Irish antiquities, signed 'Flann MacAodhegan', who professed to come from the village of Flannmacaodhegan ('mirabile dictu!')[19] in the county of Tipperary. The title page of this production displays the imprimatur of Malachy, Archbishop of Tuam, dated Galway, Kalends of December, 1636, and of Richard, Bishop of Kildare. Among the others are fragments of the Annals of Ireland; 'Lebhar Iris na Domhneill', the book of O'Donnell's Poems – Jacobite relics brimful of love and romance, and yet displaying a weird and melancholy spirit peculiar to the Irish harp; the theological works of Richard, Archdeacon of Kilkenny; St Bernard's Panegyric of St Malachi, with a portrait of the distinguished Irish prelate; Essays by Laurence O'Dolan, who facetiously called himself 'the Gentleman Friar'; and a large map of the battle of Fontenoy, supposed to have been drawn on the morning of the fray, and giving the names of the chief combatants, among whom, strange to say, none of our countrymen figure.[20] The author of this map must, like Voltaire, have had a rabid antipathy to the 'mere Irish'. It would be impossible for me in the limited space at my disposal to enumerate all these Irish MSS in the Burgundian section. Suffice it to say, that they would well repay the inspection of any Irish tourist who may be spending a holiday in Brussels. Unlike most other Old World MSS, they are not, however, illuminated to any appreciable extent. Art does not seem to have been patronised with anything like the same zeal in the cloisters of St Anthony's, where most of these relics were penned by the untiring monks. I may add here that when St Anthony's College was broken up these MSS were transferred to the Jesuit house in Mechlin, and from thence to the Brussels Royal Library, where, I am glad to say, they form very palatable literary pabulum for Flemish and German scholars.

Not a stone's throw from the Library lies the spot in the Rue Royale where an Irishman (who apologised for being one on the plea that a man born in a stable was not necessarily a horse), the Duke of Wellington, tripped it on the light fantastic toe a few evenings before the battle of Waterloo. A discussion took place a few years ago in the press between certain learned authorities regarding the precise topography of the ball-room; but the weight of logic in the argument lay with those who contended that the entertainment was held in a shed to the rere of one of the houses of the street in question. The ball was given by the Duchess of Richmond, one of the then leading belles of Brussels society. How faithfully Byron must have put on record the romance of that scene of pleasure in the following lines:

There was a sound of revelry by night,
And Belgium's capital had gathered then
Her beauty and her chivalry, and bright
The lamps shone on fair women and brave men:
A thousand hearts beat happy; and when
Music arose with its voluptuous swell,
Soft eyes look'd love to eyes that spake again,
And all went merry as a marriage bell!

Waterloo, which is situation some ten miles from Brussels, is a favourite resort of British tourists. Wagonettes ply every morning from the Hotel d'Angleterre and other inns to the historic field, and return in the evening. Before the visitor has time to take a look at his surroundings, and go back in fancy to that eventful June day in 1815, he is actually set upon by a horde of relic-vendors and guides, who jabber and shriek in a mongrel dialect, half Flemish, half English. Of relics there is a glorious and, it appeared to me, an ever-growing superabundance. Among those that fetch fancy prices I may enumerate such valuable knick-knacks as a nail from the heel of Wellington's boot; an imitation gold button from the uniform of Blucher; one of the 'sole surviving' feathers in Grouchy's cocked hat; and a half-decayed grinder of Napoleon the First! The 'Little Corporal', by the by, must have had a colossal jaw, for no less than a thousand of his grinders have been sold on the plain of Waterloo since 1815; and as for the number of Wellington nails, they would keep an ordinary shoemaker in stock in that article for the length of his natural life; while Blucher buttons and Grouchy feathers are, to use a very hackneyed but a no less expressive platitude, more numerous than the autumn leaves of Valambrossa.

Human credulity must be a fathomless ocean in very deed; for nobody – not even the most brazen-faced of relic vendors – has as yet sounded its depths. A man may be the cream of astuteness at home; he may not be caught by any amount of chaff or birdlime among his own; but give him a Gladstonian bag and send him to 'foreign parts' and you will see how naively confiding the animal becomes. He will laugh to scorn the authenticity of a relic of Brian Boru that may be shown him in the neighbourhood of Kinkora, but if the collarbone of Julius Caesar be submitted to his inspection in the Roman Forum he may be wheedled into believing it to be genuine, and may actually put down a fiver or two to get possession of the trumpery article! And then – O ye heavens! – what a locust of guides broods over Waterloo! What unmitigated gibberish falls from their perpetually wagging tongues! 'Me vill show Monsieur', lisps one, 'de house of Paris vere Vellington did coucher before de battle!' 'Do Monsieur vish', chimes in a second, 'to view de tomb of de Marquis of Anglesey's leg?' A third, if he suspects you of entertaining any anti-British proclivities, will volunteer to point you the spot where the Old Guard of Napoleon died but did not surrender. These guides, I may here parenthetically observe, are as cunning as foxes. If you happen to be a German, they will pass a glowing panegyric on Blucher – at the rate of a penny per line! If you be a loyal subject of her British Majesty, Wellington's praises will be sounded, subject to a similar tariff. Should you have the tongue and the air of a spruce Parisian dandy, these wretches will actually shed crocodile tears over the defeat of the mighty Napoleon. In fact they are, in the happy words of St Paul, 'all things to all men.' Apropos of the nether limb of the Marquis (which had to be amputated in the house of M. Paris on the field after the battle), the boot that encased the noble foot is still preserved under the old roof tree, and brings in a goodly revenue to the proprietor who charges each visitor a franc entrance fee for its inspection; while the leg itself lies in state within a lordly coffin in a grave honoured with a monument and an epitaph beneath the branches of a weeping willow! Waterloo is situated on the outskirts of the forest of Soigne, which Byron erreneously called Ardennes, and is a straggling and commonplace village. The house opposite the village church, in which the Duke of Wellington took up his head-quarters, is, I believe, still in existence, and has been for over a half a century a kind of English Mecca for English tourists in Belgium. [. . .]

After a few weeks' sojourn in the Belgian capital, I proceeded to Landen – a spot which will be always associated in history with the name of Patrick Sarsfield[21] – a dreary, desolate locality, reminding one of the Roman Campagna in miniature, with its apparently end-less plains, its tangled brushwood and its uninviting wastes. Its utter solitude is barely relieved by a few scattered elm trees, bare of trunk, that gather themselves at the summit into umbrella roofs. The river Gette flows past as lazily as the Schelde, while the only bustle of life that breaks in on the grave-like silence all around is the snort or whistle of the steam engine as the train moves by. Landen is on the rail line from Liège to Velm. If the tourist takes ticket from Brussels or Louvain to the latter town, he will have the advantage of passing by the outskirts of the battle scene, and taking notes at his leisure, for Belgian trains jog along in a Paddy-go-easy fashion that seems to suit the phlegmatic temperament of the average Fleming. A rough hewn cross still marks the spot where the decisive combat of the day was fought and where, according to tradition, Sarsfield received what afterwards turned out to be his death-wound. A visit to Landen, despite its forbidding aspect, is assuredly one of the most inter-esting pilgrimages that could be made by any Irishman who finds himself in the heart of Flanders.

BRUGES, YPRES AND OTHER BELGIAN TOWNS

Bruges is another of those old continental towns that live more in the past than in the present. Its former grandeur contrasts singu-larly with its actual decay and decrepitude. Its streets are now for the most part dreary wildernesses of bricks and mortar, while the green grass grows lustily on its lonely quays, and a silence as of the grave broods over the fallen city. [. . .] Some four hundred years ago Bruges was a most prosperous and commercial centre. The dark, grim palaces of the past remain, but they look more like mausoleums than hospitable homesteads; and indeed they are the mausoleums where the pristine glory of Bruges lies interred for ever.[22] [. . .]

I know of no sight so dismal as that of a decaying city. The wreck of genius in hoary old age is a very sad spectacle to behold; but the wreck of a once powerful aggregate of citizens is sadder still. And yet these continental towns have for the day-dreamer a peculiar charm even in their senility, for the dead walls and mouldering arches speak sermons to him who has eyes to see and ears to hear. Longfellow himself felt the spell of this witchery when he walked these desolate streets and stood under the belfry of 'this quaint old Flemish city'. The inn near the cathedral in which the American poet heard the wondrous carillon and wrote that wondrous poem[23] of his is still pointed out, while the grave of John Van Eyck, marked with a painted plaster cast of the illustrious painter and situated almost opposite the Hotel de Ville, is the object of many a pilgrimage.

The Cathedral is, externally, an uncouth edifice, but it is certainly in its interior the handsomest church in Flanders. Magnificent paintings from the brushes of Peter Porbus, Van Oost and others deck the walls; while on either side of the high altar is a fine marble tomb, symbolical of death. This cathedral, or, as it is called, 'L'Eglise St Sauveur', ought to be visited by every Irishman who finds himself in Flanders; for within its sacred precincts a portion of the mantle of Brigid, the Irish Saint, has been religiously preserved for centuries. The relic is to be found in a chapel in a south aisle on the Gospel side of the altar. There is a niche in the wall of this chapel having a small frame, with folding doors, in which the treasure is deposited.

I am indebted to the Rev. William Brady for some interesting facts concerning this Irish souvenir. From his statement it appears that in the church of St Donatus, formerly the Cathedral of Bruges, an edifice which was destroyed by revolutionary fanatics, was found a leaden or zinc plate on which is written a short account of the life of Gunelda, daughter of Godwin Count of Essex, Sussex, and Kent, and sister of Harold, the last of the Saxon Kings of England. After the Battle of Hastings she and her mother fled from Exeter in ships of Bruges and found shelter in Flanders. She died in 1087, leaving a magnificent set of jewels to the chapter of St Donatus, together with this relic of St Brigid. Her tomb in the cloisters of the church was violated by the French Republicans in 1804, when the plate was found under the head of the princess and was fortunately saved from destruction.

The plate is kept in the sacristy of St Sauvers. The most ancient account we have, except the one on the leaden plate of the relic, is to be found in an inventory of relics preserved in the church of St Donatus, and written about the year 1300. This inventory is now printed, and can be seen in Vol. III of a learned work entitled, 'Le Beffroi'. It says that in the fourteenth century this tunic was set in a precious reliquary having the form of a mantle. This cloak reliquary is mentioned in an inventory of objects given by the chapter of St Donatus to the care of Giles of Ghent, cure and sacristan of the church, the 8th of August, 1347, under this designation – 'Item, Mantellum Beate Brigid.' It may be added that in 1866 this relic was extracted and placed in its present reliquary.

In Bruges, as well as in other towns and cities of Belgium, there are convents where Irish nuns or novices reside and where young ladies from Ireland receive their education. The Ursuline Order is most patronised by our fair countrywomen. This order was founded by St Angela Merico at Bresica, in Italy, about the year 1537. It was introduced into Canada as early as 1639, and into the United States in 1727. One of these convents where the Irish most do congregate is that of Thildonck. A very amiable young lady correspondent of mine, who studied in this establishment, has been good enough to furnish me with some interesting details on the subject, from which I learn that Thildonck was founded just one century ago. The little village in which the convent is situated is some sixty miles from Antwerp, and is approached by Malins or Mechlin. It developed from being a small shed into a magnificent building, capable of sheltering some six hundred inmates, and is now the mother convent of the Ursuline convents in Belgium.

The community consists of one hundred nuns, the majority of whom are told off to teach, as the order is a purely educational one, the lay sisters acting as domestics and looking after the various farms belonging to the establishment. Assembled within its scholastic walls are pupils of almost every nationality – English blondes and French brunettes, blue-eyed, dark-haired Irish maidens, and dark-eyed, dark-haired Italians; Scotch of the rousse or auburn tint, and German gretchens of the flaxen; cream-skinned Austrians and large-orbed damsels from the glowing lap of the East; while the West Indies and North and South America contribute their quota to this galaxy of budding womanhood. The secular educational training is of a very high order of merit, comprising as it does the French, English, German, Flemish, and Italian languages, and musical morceaux from the great masters. Besides these accomplishments the girls are taught to acquire others; and dainty, tapering fingers may be seen from day to day actively engaged in needlework of every description, or etching promising pictures on canvas. The gymnastics department is also well attended to on the wise principle of the necessity of having 'mens sana in corpore sano'. Though, of course, Thildonck is a Catholic convent, there are a number of Protestant ladies educated within its walls. At one time it had on its roll no less than one hundred and fifty English-speaking pupils, the vast majority of whom belonged to the so-called Reformed Church. No distinction is, however, made between girls of various creeds. All without exception go to the Catholic chapel in the convent, in which Mass is celebrated at 6 a.m. and Benediction is given every evening. Attached to the convent is a chaplain known as 'Monsieur le Directeur', who has the spiritual control of the flock. It may not be out of place to mention here that no attempt is made to interfere with the religious beliefs of any of the pupils who are not Catholics, while the parents of these latter always receive due notice that if they sent their children to the convent, the rules and regulations of the establishment must be obeyed by them as well as by others. An English head-mistress gives instruction every morning in English to the pupils of the lower classes, who do not know French sufficiently well to allow them to attend the French classes. These little strangers, however, pick up a smattering of the Gallic tongue in a month or two, and after the lapse of a year can babble in it with as much volubility as minxes from Montmartre.

The number of pupils averages three hundred. These are divided into three sections, known respectively as 'les grandes', 'les moyennes' and 'les petites' – the old, middle-aged, and young of the girlish community. Each section occupies different parts of the school, and has its own teachers, play-grounds, and apartments [. . .]. The scholastic life here is the essence of regularity, each day being fully occupied. The pupils rise at 5 a.m. in the summer, and at 5.30 a.m. in the winter, and always retire to rest at 8 p.m. These Flemish convents stand usually in grounds beautifully laid out. They are also provided with large orchards, and thus the house is kept well supplied with fruit throughout the entire year. Once a week the pupils make an excursion into the neighbouring country, attended by three or four of the sisters. On different occasions also dramatic performances take place in the large 'salle', in which the entire community assembles to witness the performances, all the roles in the piece being filled by the pupils, some of whom may possibly become theatrical stars in after years.

In my rambles throughout Belgium I have visited not a few of these conventual establishments, and I can safely state that they are perfect in their way from every point of view. The 'pension' required is hardly one-half of the amount demanded in similar establishments at home, while they afford to young ladies the additional advantage of acquiring a profound knowledge of at least one of the foreign languages. I was glad to observe that the proportion of Irish pupils in these establishments is very considerable.

When I happened to be sojourning in St Frond a few other students and myself secured permission from the director of the seminary on St Patrick's morning to have a day's 'outing' in the town. Having heard that there were a number of our fair compatriots in the convent over the way, we proceeded at once to pay our 'devoirs' to the interesting exiles. Our little group represented on the occasion the four provinces of Ireland. One who could have qualified for a commission in the battalions of Finn if he had lived in that romantic age, for his frame was taller than a Roman spear, came from the hills of Kerry; another hailed from the town of Belfast, a third was a son of the Marble City,[24] and another had seen the light for the first time on the shores of Clew Bay, in the West. We had come from all points of the Irish compass. Wending our way through the antique streets of St Frond, each of us having a buttonhole provided with a shamrock fresh from the Irish land, we adjourned to a quiet hotel and conscientiously drowned the trefoil in a beaker of Holland's gin. Our gaiety on the occasion was somewhat damped by the fact that there was no Irish dew available for the wetting ceremony, one of our number having written too late in the month to his friends in Ireland for a black bottle of Jameson's. We, however, made the best of a bad bargain, and were as merry under the circumstances as strangers can well be in a strange land. After one or two customary toasts were disposed of we sauntered out into the Flemish country, visiting the points of interest all around and inhaling the fresh breezes of illimitable plains. Our promenade over, we wended our way to the convent, and asked to see the Irish ladies. The Superioress, after much difficulty, consented to the interview, which took place in the parlour, the only condition imposed being that the conversation should be held in either French, or, if in English, in presence of several of the English-speaking nuns of the community. Shortly afterwards, a bevy of most bewitching damsels burst on our ravished sight. They were all kindly Irish of the Irish, and each pretty bust was decked with a shamrock. The greeting, I need hardly add, was most cordial on both sides. We found that they, too, came from the four points of the Irish compass; and the merriest hour in a lifetime was spent on that occasion in wit, laughter,and repartee, even though we were throughout all these moments under the active surveillance of several sisters.

The Irish girls, however, were not entirely happy at the beginning of the interview. They had a grievance, and a very serious grievance it was, particularly when it was explained to us by the prettiest of rosebud lips we had ever seen. From time immemorial – so runs the platitude – the Irish pupils at St Frond Convent had been permitted to celebrate St Patrick's Day in the establishment by parties, in which tea and bonbons formed the creature comforts. This year, however, the permission was refused on the plea that the German girls insisted on having a festivity on the German national anniversary, the Belgians on the Belgian and the Italians on the Italian! Why, said these coy damsels – why will the Irish girls have all the fun, and we have none? So in order to obviate the possibility of confusion becoming more confounded, the good mother superioress decided on abolishing all national fetes in the establishment. We, of course, sympathised with the Mobes from Innisfail, one of whom archly confessed at the close of the meeting that our visit made more than amends for the suppression of their conventual gala. [. . .]

Ypres is a drowsy town, its streets and alleys being comparatively deserted despite the fact that it shelters some fifteen thousand inhabitants. It was at one time a very large commercial centre, when its hardy burghers numbered 200,000 souls and 4,000 looms worked merrily away within its walls. The two only memorials of its past grandeur are the Town Hall and the Benedictine Convent. Of the former building there is nothing particular to be said. The Benedictine Convent was founded in 1612 and was endowed by James II's Queen for the daughters of the Irish officers who followed her husband's fortunes in Ireland as well as in France. This convent was one of three nunneries established on the Continent, the remaining two being the Dominican convent of Lisbon, and that of Brussels, of the same order. The little chapel in Ypres is a veritable 'bijou' of ecclesiastical architecture in its interior – rich with ornaments and brilliant with frescoes from master hands. For years and years, over the mahogany stalls in this miniature sanctuary hung suspended the tattered banners of England – the trophies won on many a glorious battlefield by the soldiers of the Irish Brigade – mute but eloquent memorials of the military prowess of our race [. . .]. The tattered banners are, however, no longer keeping watch and ward by the tabernacle; and the Irish nuns themselves have almost altogether passed away. Where the conquered banners, hung up by Murrough O'Brien 'as an offering to God and Fatherland', are lying at present, I cannot say; but on the floor which has been appropriately called 'the roof of an Irish necropolis' we can still read the names of Dame Margaret Arthur, Madame Butler, Dame Marie Benedicte Dalton, Dame Marie Scholastique Lynch, Dame Marie Bernard Lynch, and Dame Marie Benedicte Byrne – the latter lady, who was born in Dublin in 1775 and died in Ypres in 1840, having been the last of a long line of Irish abbesses of the convent. When Leo XIII was Nuncio at Brussels it is recorded that he paid a visit to the Irish abbey at Ypres, and dedicated a small chapel in the convent garden on that occasion. A few years ago the reception of the last Irish novice, a Miss Kearney, took place within the historic edifice.[25]

Not very far from Ypres lies the village of Ramillies, the scene of the famous battle between the Duke of Marlborough and the Marshal de Villeroy [. . .]. Anglo-Irish soldiers met their Franco-Irish countrymen on many a field in France and Flanders.[26] Even in the throes of the great French Revolution Irishmen were found on both sides, for there were Irish Royalists as well as Irish Red Republicans. O'Connell, a student at St Omer's, was a sympathiser with the Bourbons; Henry Sheares[27] was an ardent advocate of the Jacobins.

The trip from Waterloo to Namur lies through what was called the 'cockpit of Europe'. And a veritable cockpit it has been for the Dutch and the Spanish, the French and the English chanticleers. This portion of Belgium ought to be proud of its historic associations, although in all probability the generations of Flemings that witnessed 'the pomp and glorious circumstances of war' in their midst considered such international duelling a frightful nuisance. The peasants who dwelt near the conflux of the Sambre and the Meuse[28] could admire Mars and Bellon disporting themselves as best they might at a respectful distance; but when the divinities put up at their village hostelries, burned down their haystack, and scuttled their granary stores, these simple, unsophisticated rustics might well be excused if they turned up their noses at the prospect of an armed engagement in their secluded valleys. And, besides, they had a perfect right to protest against the injustice of having their portion of Flanders turned into an arena for the bloody sport of European gladiators. Why should they become the scapegoats of the Great Powers? What under heaven had they to do with the feuds that may crop up between the Saxon and the Gaul? [. . .]

Namur itself is the capital of the province of that name and is a strong fortress, with a population of some 30,000. [. . .] Namur, it may be added, is also famous in Irish annals as being one of the resting places of the O'Donnells and O'Neills in their pilgrimage to Rome; while modern records tell us that it was one of the favourite resorts of Charles Lever during his residence in Belgium. The Irish novelist had, however, his fixed home in Brussels, where he penned his two best works of fiction, *Harry Lorrequer* and *Charles O'Malley*, in 1840, '41 and '42.

The author of these rollicking Irish tales was at the time physician to the British Embassy, and an intimate boon companion of Sir H. Seymour, the Minister to Leopold's Court. Lever was just then a very prominent figure in the social world of the Belgian capital. His charming conversational powers, his innate grace of manners and deportment, and his growing fame as a litterateur opened to him the doors of many an eclectic salon. Lever was, moreover, like Moore,[29] one of those dainty commoners who dearly love a lord, and who think themselves unspeakably happy if they can rub their skirts against the purple robes of the princes, kings and Grand Moguls of the age. There are some eyes that are wonderfully fascinated by the sight of family trees of an antediluvian stem; there are other orbs that are democratically blind to the beauties of such spectacles. The question of taste is an open one, and is destined to remain an open one to the end of time. Lever, however, did not confine his society to the Patrician nobodies of his day in Brussels. He devoted many of his hours to companionship with literary lions; for the aristocracy of talent – which is, after all, the only aristocracy worthy of the name – had its charms for one who was himself a member of that select circle. Just about that epoch Brussels used to receive periodical visits from Dumas père,[30] the head of the fiction-factory known as 'Dumas et Compagnie', who had the habit of earning twenty pounds a day and spending forty. Dumas and Lever met and, being both Freemasons in literature, fraternised. As the author of *Charley O'Malley* had all the emotional qualities – the wit, the passion and the verve of the genuine Gaul – it is no wonder that he made a very favourable impression on the whole-souled though erratic Frenchman. Lever's Irish yarns, spun in tolerably good French, must have been peculiarly palatable to Dumas, who loved to listen to the drollest of stories. Our Irish novelist had also at the same time the privilege of dining at the same table with Monsignore Pecci, who in our day was elevated to the curule chair in the Catholic Church as Leo XIII. Monsignore Pecci was then Papal Legate at Brussels and in that capacity attended the Ambassadorial dinners at which Lever was always a welcome guest. The present Pontiff, I am informed, still cherishes lively and agreeable souvenirs of his chats with the Irish litterateur. [. . .] The only other Irish association connected with Namur is the diocesan seminary of the town, where up to a few years ago at least a few ecclesiastical students from Ireland used to be trained for the priesthood.

Not very far from Namur the traveller happens on Huy, a town which also has its Irish associations. Huy boasts a population of 8,000 and is situated in a picturesque site on the banks of the Meuse. The old citadel, dating back hundreds of years, has been remodelled on the approved plan of modern fortifications, and commands the passage of the valley of the Meuse, quite close to the Abbey of Neufmoustier, which was founded by Peter the Hermit on his return from the first crusade and the capture of Jerusalem in 1115. The remains of the great Russian were at first interred in this sacred edifice, but they were removed to Rome in 1643. The abbey itself has long since disappeared, but a portion of the cloisters still remains. The peculiar interest which Huy must have for every Irish tourist is derived from the fact that it was within its walls that the indomitable Sarsfield breathed his last. It is always cruel to dispel a sweet illusion; but the cruelty is often necessary in the interests of historical truth. Some of my readers have, no doubt, been trained to believe that Sarsfield fell on the field of Landen, exclaiming – 'Oh, would that this blood of mine were for Ireland!' Tradition tells us that he used these words; John Banim endorses the traditional account in his 'Boyne Water', and Thomas Davis emphasises its accuracy; but, after all, tradition cannot in such matters be depended on with very much security. It is, however, historically certain that Sarsfield did not expire on the field of Landen, as from 'Les Lettres Historiques, 1693', as well from other equally authentic sources, we learn that Lucan, whose name was originally given in the list of the dead on the evening of the battle, was just then only wounded, and that he was on the following day removed on a litter to Huy, where he died. [. . .]

Ostend is another of those Belgian towns that can boast some Irish historical associations, for it was during several years the home of over a score of Franco-Irish soldiers who were exiled from France by the Revolutionary party for their unswerving loyalty to the Royalist cause. These soldiers, bearing such names as Blake, Burke, O'Donnell and Dillon, were, like most of their fellow-countrymen who had taken up arms under the Bourbons, very staunch adherents of King Louis. In other words, they were Monarchists or Loyalists to the very marrow of their bones. For the Lilies of France they would gladly risk everything, even life itself; but when the 'Fleur de Lys' lost its once magic power and was replaced by the Tricolour, they had no opportunity of doing it yeoman service any longer. Proscribed in the land of their forefathers and expelled from the land of their adoption, these Irishmen waited patiently here in Ostend for the return of the Bourbons to Versailles. [. . .] They would not join the battalions of the Republic; and even when Napoleon burst like a meteor on the European firmament they were not dazzled by his lustre, for he, too, represented the growing power and influence of the new epoch that refused to acknowledge a Bourbon regime. They had all the passionate faith of that romantic troubadour who used to go about from prison door to prison door singing, 'O Charles! O mon Roi!' in the hope that the long-lost Dauphin would start from his mystic dungeon, as if by magic, and return in triumph to the throne of his ancestors. Years and years passed away, and the Bourbons and their aristocracy still roamed over Europe, depending on the charity of European monarchs for a wretched subsistence. At last, in 1814, their exile came to an end. Five venerable Irishmen left Ostend in that year for Paris – the remnants of the score of Irish exiles who had taken refuge in that Belgian town in 1793. All the others had crossed the mysterious Rubicon before they could set foot on French soil, or take their stand once more under the Bourbon banner.

Ostend is now a very fashionable watering-place, to which English tourists usually go in the summer months to be fleeced. The fleecing process is nearly always borne by these gentry with the utmost good humour, for Toms and Dicks and 'Arries do not expect to share the championship of perfumed counts and chevaliers at a continental 'table d'hôte' without paying the piper for such a very special privilege. Moreover, when an Anglo-Saxon bank clerk goes to Antwerp for a fortnight's holiday, and gets introduced to the daughter of a Russian prince or the widow of a Spanish grandee, and takes promenades on the beach with such stately stems of the old nobility, must he not spend an odd louis off and on in purchasing bouquets or investing in bonbons for the petted darlings? Does not his plebeian heart expand with tremulous delight throughout these mild flirtations with the daughters of the gods? True it is that when he has reached the end of his purse he will find himself deserted by these arch beauties, and a glimmering suspicion may flash on his mind that they may be trumpery articles after all, and that he has fallen a victim of sirens originally reared in the slums of Paris, Berlin or Vienna; for wherever one discovers a casino, there one is always sure to hit on a veritable mine of bogus aristocratic ore. In a week's stay in Ostend I was introduced to no less than a score of counts and a baker's dozen of live marquises. Their ancestors, they told me, won their spurs and parchments as Crusaders in the Holy

Land, and the blood of each of them was as pure – so I was informed – as the purest drop circulating in the veins of a Howard or a Montmorency. When, however, one of these noble lords, after dilating on the grandeur of his ancestry, would wind up by asking the loan of a ten-franc piece, 'just till tomorrow, you know', I became slightly incredulous, and kept a firm grip of my silver. I did not believe then, nor do I believe now, in the theory of stumping up in hard cash in order to be graciously allowed to come between the fragant nobility of these people and the wind.

Despite this locust of adventurers there are, however, a goodly number of genuine Belgian nobles and their families to be found in Ostend during the season. These latter follow the Court as chickens follow the mother hen. While King Leopold and his spouse reside in Laeken these butterflies of fashion disport themselves on the slopes of the Montagne de la Cour in Brussels, within ten minutes' drive of the Palace; but when Royalty takes up its bed and whisks itself off to Ostend, as it does annually, all the courtiers follow suit, for it would be a crime against the canons of respectability to be seen in the streets of Brussels at a time when Royalty is taking its bath elsewhere. King Leopold himself is rather brilliant in society. Men who are not overburdened with ability usually are; and Leopold has not yet signalised himself in any particular way either as a ruler or a diplomatist. His wife, however, does for him anything that is going about in the shape of government or political intrigue, just as Marie Antoinette used to do while her stupid lord was blowing the bellows in the Royal smithy of Versailles. Marriage in such cases cannot be pronounced a failure, for wives like these possess far more than the ordinary market value. [. . .] The King and Queen may be seen any evening during the season walking by the Digne, a wall some forty feet high and half a mile in length, which extends from the sea to the ramparts. It is a kind of public promenade, and commands a wide extent of dunes and flat sands to the sea. On the beach are some one hundred bathing machines, while the 'plage' is crowded with bathers of both sexes, 'decorously clad', as the formula goes, in tight-fitting bathing costumes.

The journey from Ostend to Ghent or Gand is not a long or wearisome one. Between Bruges and the latter town lies a grand canal, bounded by high banks on either side, lined with tall trees, and graced by the presence of beautiful villas and well-kept gardens. It may be remembered that Dante, in his 'Inferno', compares the embankment which separated the River of Tears from the Sandy Desert with that which the Flemings have thrown up between Bruges and Ghent against the assaults of the sea. [. . .] Ghent has a certain interest for the Irish tourist, derived from the fact that the Church of St Nicholas in that city is the last resting-place of one of the most patriotic of the Irish Bishops of the Penal Days, the Right Rev. Nicholas French, of Ferns. It was in that quaint old town where the whole-souled prelate passed his declining years, exiled from the land of his birth. His remains were placed at the foot of the grand altar of St Nicholas. A slab of the purest marble, decorated with a cardinal's hat and armorial bearings, contains a touching as well as a truthful inscription to his memory. St Nicholas's is one of the most ancient of Flemish churches, and was at one time a necropolis for the celebrities of the epoch, just as the Cathedral of St Bavon was, where one still sees in a subterranean chapel the tombs of Hubert Van Eyck and his beautiful sister, also a painter, who refused several flattering offers of marriage in order, as she said, to consecrate herself wholly to the cult of art. [. . .]

The valley of the Schelde, in which the historic village of Fontenoy is situated, is pleasant enough to the view, particularly if one looks more after the pastoral than the purely picturesque in nature. It is a quiet agricultural nook, where turnips and potatoes grow in abundance, and where vetches actually run riot in all directions. And yet we are here in very close proximity to the mining districts, alive with rope-walks, tan-yards, limekilns, and safety lamps, where thousands pass their lives away without having been able to gaze even once on the noonday sun. Odd guffaws of smoke, borne on the eddying breeze, greet the traveller in these secluded plains, reminding him of the presence of the collieries and iron foundries hard by; and in the evening one may encounter a group of prematurely old men with coal-black faces and lowering brows passing moodily on. These unfortunate miners seem to have lost all bouyancy of spirits. The milk of human kindness – if it were admissible that they ever had any – must have been changed to gall – so much so, in fact, that they rarely converse with each other when the hard day's work is over. They enjoy no relaxation properly so-called, and their pent-up feelings have therefore no safety-valve at their command, save at those very rare intervals when they rush up in despair from the bowels of the earth and take up arms against capital, burning down the warehouses and spreading destruction far and wide with the force and frenzy of lunatics. On occasions such as these the entire district becomes a scene of civil war. Socialist emissaries from Paris and Berlin plan these periodical rebellions. They gather the miners in dozens in dark places, and speak to them in bated breath of the wrongs they suffer; they tell them that the only remedy for their galling ills is a general rising against society. They point to the gleaming axe and the blazing torch as the ready instruments of vengeance; and then, when they have worked up the toilers to a proper pitch of indignation, they discreetly retire from the scene, leaving their victims to battle as best they can with the military forces of the Crown. And then, of course, the usual run of events takes place. Some of the miners are shot down like dogs, a few hundred others are sent to prison, while the remainder return, cowed, cuffed, and submissive, to the mines. And so the grim farce ends for the moment, till the next opportunity comes the way and the next holocaust is effected.

Fontenoy lies some five miles south-east of Tournay, on the old post road to Ath, near the village of Bourquembrays. It is a straggling hamlet, comprising some twenty or twenty-five low-sized cottages, the red-tiled roofs of which give them a somewhat picturesque appearance. A little antique church, flanked by a solemn graveyard, stands at the cross-roads in the very centre of the village. [. . .] Here any microscopic mound one might meet with is called a hill by the peasantry; and if there happened to be a decently-sized hill in the vicinity I have no doubt that it would be turned by them into a mountain, for Belgians, living for the most part in a country which is as flat as the Bog of Allen, fall into the natural mistake of making pyramids out of molehills. A Fleming who never saw a mountain in his life is often to be met with as a Tipperaryman who never saw the sea. [. . .]

It was in the autumn of 1878 that I paid a flying visit to Fontenoy. I was lucky enough on my arrival to be introduced to a centenarian – a veteran who had served in the Grand Armee of Napoleon, and who was delighted to find a fresh listener to the story of his past exploits. The aged soldier told me that he was for years in receipt of a daily allowance of two and a-half francs for services rendered on the battlefield. 'It is enough', he said, 'for my modest wants; for an old militaire like myself lives more on the memory of the past than he does on a two-sou loaf.' Garrulity is one of the weakneses of old age, and the veteran was of course exceedingly garrulous. I let him have his way, for his narrative was unusually interesting. After having given me a vivid account of his campaigns under the Great Napoleon, winding up with the disastrous battle of Waterloo, the aged soldier broke forth into expressions of burning enthusiasm when he spoke of the martial powers of the Emperor and the fascinating influence which he exercised over his battalions. 'Ah, voyez vous', he cried, 'I could have died for him! And when he was taken off by the English to St Helena something inspired me with the idea that he would come back once more and put himself at the head of his children. Did he not return from Elba? And why should he not return from St Helena? And so I waited for many and many a year, always on the look-out for my emperor. When the news of his death appeared in the newspapers, I would not believe it. I said, 'Napoleon is not dead; he shall come back.' And when they told me that the hero's remains were later on transferred to the Invalides of Paris, I thought the story a fable and was still incredulous. It is only of late that I doubt that he still lives. And if he came back to-day, he would not, alas! find two of his old Guard surviving to give him the old familiar military salute!' The veteran's eyes swam in tears and his voice grew husky with emotion as he concluded.

I might observe that this man was not by any means the only one of Napoleon's troops who had an unshaken faith in their master's return for years after he had passed away. An anecdote is told of Prince Jerome Bonaparte that goes to confirm this fact. Jerome was from thirty to forty years of age a living image of his immortal uncle in the flesh. He had the eyes and the features of the Little Corporal; and he wore no beard or moustaches in order to make the resemblance more striking. Long years after the hero of Austerlitz had been gathered to his forefathers, Jerome was proceeding on a tour of pleasure through a little hamlet in the South of France. He was mounted on a white horse, and, passing through the square, he saw a group of veterans armed with crutches who, the moment they gazed on him, raised an enthusiastic shout of welcome, crying out, 'Vive l'Empereur', and fairly beside themselves with joy at the idea that the idol of their hearts was back once more on his native land! These veterans were, like many others, fixed in their belief that their great captain would start some day, even if it were from his ashes, to lead them on again to glory and to victory.

Standing at the outskirts of Fontenoy, the old soldier pointed me out De Barri's wood and St Antoing in the distance, and recounted in sympathetic terms the story of the famous battle.[31] A granduncle of his fought that day under the banners of the Marshal de Saxe. A traditional account of the conflict passed from generation to generation in his family. He spoke in warm and admiring accents of the 'brave Irish, without whom we', he said, 'would have had to retreat ingloriously from the field on that occasion.' 'The Irish' he observed, later on, 'had always a chivalrous love for France, and I have often felt aggrieved that France does not appreciate that affection better. We have only given Ireland Hoche and Humbert and a few battalions; Ireland has given us half a million of men, who died in defence of our country.' And so we chatted and chatted till the evening came on, when I was compelled to return to Tournay. A short time afterwards I was informed that the venerable warrior had passed away. His dying words were still, 'Long live the Emperor!' [. . .]

ILLUSTRIOUS IRISHMEN IN BELGIUM

There is but scanty material in existence regarding the lives of several Irishmen who were in the their day rather prominent figures in the Lowlands, and whose names are now quite forgotten in the land of their birth and ancestry. It was only in a haphazard excursion through the pages of an old encyclopedia in the Brussels Royal Library that I discovered some of the data which I give in this paper, the remainder having been furnished me by Monsieur Everarts, a distinguished Flemish archaeologist, whom I knew in Louvain to have taken such a deep interest in everything Irish that I actually caught him on many occasions in the act of poring studiously over the pages of a Gaelic grammar! To this gentleman I am indebted for some very important and hitherto unpublished information regarding a few Irish footprints on the Continent which I purpose laying under contribution later on. I may add that I have never met a foreigner who could rival this talented and industrious scholar in the knowledge of Irish history and of Irish Jacobite literature. To meet such an entertaining gentleman in the byways or on the highways of life abroad is, I fancy, ample compensation for the misfortune of having once encountered a Knight of the Legion of Honour (and a Bachelor of the Sorbonne to boot) who once asked me why Ireland did not put up with police rule just as the other remaining shires of England did! What a pull-down for our national *amour propre*, surely, to hear our country referred to as if she were as much part and parcel of England as York or Kent! There are, however, Continental scholars by the hundred who could teach this chevalier many a sound and solid lesson in Irish geography.

Of the illustrious Irishmen who settled down in Belgium, Dr John Sinnich is the best known, and may be ranked, perhaps, as the foremost. This eminent divine was born in West Cork in one of the opening years of the seventeenth century. Like many others of our race in that day, he was compelled to seek for education in a foreign land, and with that object in view he entered Louvain University, where he soon won the highest of honours. In the old records of that establishment I find him referred to in very flattering Middle Age Latin as an Hibernian scholar, whose thesis for a doctorate in theology in the 'aula maxima' was listened to with admiring attention by the most distinguished savants of Flanders. After having secured the cap, Dr Sinnich was appointed to a theological chair in the university, and was known in the town as 'le célèbre Irlandais'. Too much learning, however, as well as too little, is a decidedly dangerous thing; for we find the doctor later on bringing down the thunderbolts of Rome on his devoted head by enouncing propositions of a suspiciously heretical character, although the formal denunciation of his theories was not made till December 1690, some thirty years after their author had passed away, when Alexander VIII occupied the chair of Peter. The learned Irishman wrote and published several tracts, the doctrines of which were patently Jansenistic.[32] Jansenius, who, by-the-by, was bishop of historic Ypres, used to receive Dr Sinnich occasionally in his palace in that town; and probably it was in the course of the conversations they had together that the Corkman became an ardent disciple of the great prelate. Dr Sinnich died in 1666, and his remains were interred in the cemetery of Louvain.

The Plunketts are another of those Irish families whose ramifications have extended to Belgium. One of these, who, I believe, belonged to the 'Hamilcar' Plunkett branch, of Rathmore and Fingal, was Joseph Plunkett, a soldier of fortune, who left Ireland after the Treaty of Limerick, and spent most of his life campaigning in Flanders. Contemporary accounts allude to him as a dashing officer, brave and chivalrous, and combining in his person the herculean proportions of the Irishman and the grace and elegance of a courtier of Versailles. After having unsheathed his sword on many a hard-fought field, he died eventually in the service of Austria in 1778. Another of the same family was Jean Joseph Ferdinand Plunkett, member of the Equestrian Order of Brabant, who was created Baron Plunkett de Rathmore by William I, King of the Low Countries, on the 8th of July, 1816, in recognition of his many and important services to the Crown as a diplomatist.

The O'Sullivans of famed Dunboy[33] have also made their mark in the Netherlands. Coming hither from the coast of Beare, in Ireland, they attained to very high positions in the military and political departments of the State. Jean Patrice O'Sullivan was one of the most distinguished public men in Belgium some fifty and odd years ago. He rose to the rank of councillor of the nation, and was appointed successively Chevalier of the Order of the Dutch Lion and member of the Equestrian Order of West Flanders. He was also a very impressive Parliamentary orator, and was one of the most popular idols of the day. Alphonse Albert Henri Comte O'Sullivan, a scion of the same stock, was born in Bruges in 1779, and was sent at an early age to Paris, where he prosecuted his studies at the Lycée Napoléon of that city. With the aid of a generous allowance from his family, he was enabled to force his way into the gilded salons of the Directory and the Empire, where he boasted of having danced on more occasions than one with the Empress Josephine. Returning to Belgium shortly afterwards, O'Sullivan was appointed representative of the Low Countries at Berlin, from which post he was promoted to that of Minister at St Petersburg, where he became the intimate friend of the Czar Nicholas, from whom he received the Cross of a Chevalier of the Order of St Anne. When the Belgian Revolution of 1830 broke out, he threw up his post under the Dutch Crown, as all his Irish sympathies went out to a people 'rightly struggling to be free'. The diplomatist became a soldier, and fought bravely on the battlements of Antwerp in the cause of Belgian independence. When at last the hardy Flemings and the bold, impetuous Wallons shook off the foreign yoke, and Leopold I was crowned King of the new-born nation, O'Sullivan's spirit of self-sacrifice and the services he rendered to the Revolution were not forgotten; for he was in 1831 sent to Vienna as the representative of Belgium, and was elevated in 1838 to the rank of Plenipotentiary Minister, when he was commissioned by his Government to repair to Constantinople in order to arrange a treaty of commerce with Turkey. His diplomacy on the banks of the Bosphorus was so pre-eminently successful that all the conditions of the Belgian Cabinet were in a few weeks subscribed to by the Sultan and his advisers. In recognition of this triumph he was immediately afterwards gazetted baron, and in due course of time his name appeared as Count O'Sullivan on the Court roll. He was also at the same period nominated Commander of the Orders of Leopold, the Sultan, and Gregory the Great. He passed away in the beginning of the fifties, loved and revered by all Belgians, who had no more faithful friend and no more devoted champion than he. His son, the second Count O'Sullivan, holds now,

I believe, a high and important post in the Belgian diplomatic service; while the Plunketts still have living representatives in the land of Flanders. [. . .]

THE BELGIAN CHARACTER AND FLEMISH SOCIAL LIFE

I have now done with Irish memorials in Belgium. Before proceeding to France in our expeditionary tour, it may not be inappropriate to say a word or two about the social aspect of the Belgian character. The Belgian character, nationally speaking, is identical; but socially it is twofold; for the common motherland owns two distinct races, who speak different tongues and follow different customs – the Flemings and the Wallons. Of the Wallons I need only say that their patois is French, as is also the natural bent of their minds. They are French in their light, airy mood, their quick discernment and their frank good nature. The Flemings bear, on the other hand, a strong resemblance to Germans, although it must be added that they are not at all so phlegmatic as the average Berliner or Bavarian.

Like the Walloon, the Fleming has the bump of patriotism well developed on his cranium – that is to say, if there be such a bump in existence, an observation which proves, by-the-way, that I can lay no claim to be considered a phrenologist. The Fleming himself is an honest, unassuming fellow. He is rough and uncouth at times, and in the humbler strata smells offensively of garlic; but take him for all in all, he is one of these men whose good qualities grow on you gradually from social intercourse and for whom you are glad to entertain an ever-increasing esteem. Not being over-scrupulously polite in his manners, neither is he vicious. Mephistopheles says, and with truth, that the society where most vice abounds is always the most polite. The Fleming's ways of life are simple and his morals could not, I dare say, be found fault with even by the rigid

Mr Stead[34] himself. Hence it is there are so few Flemings in that rather numerous brood of well-dressed adventurers and titled pick-pockets who infest the leading capitals of Europe. Flanders may have its footpads, who will honestly and above-board knock you over, and relieve you of your hard cash; but it cannot produce the dainty and the perfumed thief, who, while bandying elegant compliments with you, manages to becomes the master of your watch and chain.

Of Flemish womankind I would speak with all due deference. The belle of the town, with her pancake-hat sitting jauntily on tresses that ripple down almost to her eyebrows, is nearly always a bewitching creature. She has not the subtle grace, the light, trivial sentimentalities or the pretty wee feet of the Parisienne; but the colour in his cheeks is healthier, her step is more elastic and her manner more natural. In the country she is plump, ruddy-faced and alluring, a nymph of the Nora Creina[35] category, whose gold and flaxen locks scorn any headgear and defy the sun. There is a remarkable similarity between the Flemish country belle and the German gretchen. Both are distinctly Teuton. Thanks to their dislike for tight-lacing, their waists have a certain well-preserved rotundity not altogether disagreeable to behold; while their deep blue eyes look like tiny round bits of azure stolen from the waters of Lake Como. The Flemish lady, however, I regret to say, has one defect. Sitting in a picturesquely languid pose for a painter or a sculptor, she may be all perfection, but when you converse with her and her tongue begins to wag, many of the charms of her beauty evaporate; for that hard and uncouth Flemish tongue of hers puckers her pretty lips into such ugly shapes that the mouth which but a moment ago was delicious, while it remained mute, now becomes a very monster of deformity. Certainly the Flemish language bears a striking resemblance to the Euscara of Spain – a dialect which, if we are to believe an old legend, gave Satan himself the lockjaw when he attempted to speak it. I fancy that in the cause of gallantry, the Belgian Parliament should pass an act making it penal on any members of the fair sex to respond to any protestations of love in that unlovely tongue. If Venus herself spoke in Flemish on Mount Ida she could never have secured the golden apple. There are cases on record in other countries where a breach of promise of marriage arose out of the mere fact of a young man happening to gaze on his fair affianced while she was doing justice to a chicken at table or plunging into the delicacies of tomato sauce – she looked so prosaically active, to be sure, on such occasions; but it is a far greater shock to the nerves of a sentimental lover, after his gushing proposal is over, to find the sweet mouth which he asked to be his falter the willing 'yaw', in the ugliest of contortions.

Flemish social life may be best appreciated at the village festivals or 'kermesses', which take place throughout the country at certain fixed intervals. Here in the fair-green we can see the merry-go-rounds; the tents where the champion athletes and the champion acrobats of Flanders astonish the native, for the consideration of a penny entrance fee; improvised theatres where fifth-rate actors and actresses perform; tournaments in which the harlequins of the gutter promenade with the majesty of monarchs; stalls where the vendors of taffy and sugar-candy are driving a roaring trade in catering for the palates of the noisy urchins and romping maidens; and the fortune-teller's wagon, in the dark and mysterious interior of which grizzly beldames whisper to the simple rustic girl the revelation that one fine morning some noble prince or some 'preux chevalier' will come to woo her and win her, and bear her away in triumph to his own gorgeous palatial halls! Maidens, whose young men are away in a garrison town doing their allotted terms of military service, step up these wagons, and earnestly ask if Jean or Jacques or François is still true to his lady-love, or if some fine dame from the city has taught him to forget the darling of his native village. And the old witch grins for a moment or two; her dry blue lips part, displaying a toothless mouth; and sometimes she answers yes, and sometimes she answers no; but her replies are, generally speaking, as vague and almost as solemn as those of the Pythoness of that far-away time in which, just as in the present, fools had to pay for their crass credulity. And then in the evening the whole green is lit up with Venetian lanterns, the band play inspiriting music and the couples whirl around to the melting measures of a waltz. Here and there the 'sabots' of the rustic girls clatter when the national dance, which is somewhat like our own jig, is struck up in the welkin, and the boys in blouse indulge in the most fantastic hops, while casting sheep's eyes on the fair partners who gyrate before them. And so, when the carillon rings out the witching hour of midnight, the music of the orchestra is hushed, the lamps are quenched and the clamour of merry laughter dies away on the green, the last of the villagers disappears into his humble home and a solemn silence reigns around.

A comparatively happy and contented race are these Flemings. In these calm Arcadian plains – we do not allude here to the mining districts – they have no grinding taskmasters to contend with, they are the sole gainers by that which the honest sweat of their brows brings them in; no Shylocks are watching around, seeking whom they may devour. Removed alike from the luxury of the rich and the penury of victimised serfs, these Flemish peasants are splendid specimens of a class that found its happiness only when it won its national independence.

Chapter 2

Northern France

SAINT OMER, DOUAI, SAINT MALO AND BRITTANY

I do not envy the Irishmen who can step for the first time on French soil without feeling his heart throb faster, or without finding himself carried back in fancy to a past that speaks so eloquently on his countrymen's military prowess under the Bourbon flag. There is something that appeals to our better nature while we are gazing on a land for which half a million of our kith and kin perished on many a battlefield throughout Europe in the last century. The records in the Ministry of War at Paris prove the authenticity of this number,[1] and give all due credit to the spirit of self-sacrifice that animated these Irish exiles in the advancement of the interests of France all over the Continent; for it must be remembered that these soldiers of our race were by no manner of means mere mercenaries. They were not, for instance, like the Swiss, who, while remaining steadfast patriots as long as they camped amid their own hills and mountains, ceased to be actuated by any such disinterested motives when they went abroad. [. . .] It was with such thoughts and associations floating in my mind that I crossed the Belgian frontier, and found myself in the sunny land of France.

After a day's rest in Lille, the first town under the Tricolour where I could discover any footprints of the Gael was Saint Omer. Here it was that Daniel O'Connell studied after his departure from the Josephite College of Louvain. Saint Omer is situated in the department of the Pas de Calais, and is a rather redoubtable fortress, its fortifications being two or three miles in circuit, while the ramparts are planted with elm trees, and look somewhat picturesque at a distance. It is a quiet old town, and although its streets are broad and its general aspect is comparatively pleasing, it looks somehow or another as if it had seen better days. And if all accounts be true, it was at one time a kind of French Clonmacnoise; for here stood the celebrated Abbey of St Bertin, the richest of the Benedictine Order (where Childeric III, the last of the Merovingian monarchs, passed away), flanked by twenty-five convents, where learning was much patronised in the so-called dark ages. The population of Saint Omer now numbers some 20,000, a genial, unassuming muster of citizens and citizenesses, the flower of whom meet twice a week in the pleasant summer evenings in the square, under the shadow of tall grey brick houses, to hear the inspiriting music of the local orchestra as it discusses a variety of airs from Rouget de l'Isle's 'Marseillaise' down to Offenbach's 'Gendarmes'. Outside the town peasant proprietors work bravely and manfully against many difficulties. They cultivate a broad extent of marshes which were drained by their hardy forefathers, the drainage having been effected by ditches forming, so to speak, a labyrinth isolating every field. Each of the farmers had a boat of his own, in which he conveys his agricultural tools and produce. This district looks to the travelled eye like a rural Venice in miniature; while the floating islands lend it at times a fairy-like aspect.

One of the few spots worth visiting in the town itself is the Rue St Bertin, where one can still see the mouldering remains of the famous abbey of that name already referred to, which was once the noblest Gothic structure in French Flanders. This abbey, it must be stated, was suppressed at the outbreak of the Revolution of 1792. The Convention, curiously enough, spared the edifice; but the officials of the Directory sold it for the materials, having unroofed and stripped it of its woodwork, while leaving the walls comparatively uninjured. Somewhere about the fifties of this century the magistrates of the town displayed the Vandal instincts within them by issuing an order that these walls should be razed to the ground on the trumpery plea that some of the unemployed workingmen in the district should get something to do. The only fragment that escaped destruction on this occasion was a stately tower, dating from the thirteenth century, in which Becket sought an asylum when he was a fugitive from England.

Before entering into the few details at my command concerning Daniel O'Connell's life at Saint Omer, it may not be out of place to give the reader a brief account of O'Connell's uncle, who was one of the most distinguished Irish officers in the service of France. This dashing 'militaire' was the youngest of twenty-two children, the issue of one marriage, and was born in Derrynane, in the county of Kerry, in the month of August 1743. Having been sent by his father, Daniel O'Connell, at the age of fourteen, to France, he received a solid education; and having preferred military life to any other, he won his first spurs during the seven years' war in Germany. When the campaign was over he became attached to a 'genie' corps, and soon became one of the leading military engineers of France. He subsequently crowned himself with glory at the siege and capture of Port Mahon, in Minorca, from the English in 1779, and was nominated, for his bravery, major in the Regiment of Royal Swedes. He had attained the rank of lieutenant-colonel in the same regiment when an unsuccessful attack was made in 1782 by the French floating batteries on Gibraltar. In this desperate assault, in which he was second in command, a portion of his ear was swept away by a ball, while a shell from the English mortars burst at his feet and inflicted no less than nine wounds on his person. After a long and almost fatal illness he recovered, and was appointed colonel-commandant of a German regiment of 2,000 men in the service of France, which he reorganised so successfully that he was shortly afterwards promoted to the responsible position of Inspector-General of all the French Infantry. Step by step O'Connell mounted from the humble position of second lieutenant to this high and respected rank without the aid of friends or patrons, and solely through his own surpassing merit.

When the French Revolution, however, overturned the Bourbon throne, O'Connell refused to serve the Republic. He would not desert the white flag of the Louis. He had the same worship of royalty which subsequently characterised his illustrious nephew, Dan – a worship which hardly knew any bounds, and which actually prompted the latter on one occasion to wade knee deep in the waters of Old Dunleary in order to welcome the last of the Georges to the shores of Ireland. The spirit of modern progress had not touched the hearts of either uncle or nephew in this respect. Monarchy, for them, remained environed in its apocryphal 'right divine' to the very end. Although O'Connell, the Military Inspector, was hard pressed by Carnot to continue his services in the same post, he absolutely declined the offer, and joined the French princes in exiles in Coblentz. In 1793, en route for Kerry, he had an interview with Pitt in London, and laid before that statesman a plan for the restoration of the Bourbon family to the French throne, which, however, had no practical effect. He was soon afterwards put in the command of an Irish Brigade of six regiments in the British service; but he virtually abandoned that post by returning in 1802 to France, where he was taken prisoner on the charge of treason, and where he remained a captive till the Bourbons came back in 1814, when he was released, and his sufferings were compensated for by a countship in parchment and a generalship in the army. He was for years subsequently a prominent figure in the Bourbon Court in Paris, where his past sacrifices in the Royalist cause were appreciated by all, and by none more than by the Duke and Duchess of Berry. When in 1830 another revolution wrecked the Bourbon craft, and Louis Philippe mounted the throne with the Tricolour, Count O'Connell refused to take the oath of fidelity to the new sovereign. He was accordingly deprived of his military rank, and retired to the country seat of his son-in-law at Madon, near Blois, on the banks of the Loire, where he passed away on the 9th of July, 1833, in his ninetieth year of his age. A contemporary French writer says of him: 'He had never in the season of his prosperity forgotten his country or his God. Loving that country with the strongest affection, he retained to the last the full use of her native language; and although master of the Spanish, Italian, German, Greek and Latin, as well as the French and English languages, it was to him a source of the greatest delight to find any person capable of conversing with him in the pure Gaelic of his native mountains.' The Count's remains lie interred in that secluded little valley of the Loire, where he spent the last three years of his eventful life.

While the uncle was winning military laurels for himself all over Europe the nephew was studying at Saint Omer. Daniel O'Connell and his younger brother had been sent to the college of that town at the expense of another uncle of theirs who resided at Derrynane. The future Repealer was about seventeen years at the time, and had the reputation of being considered one of the cleverest boys in his class. [. . .] The college where O'Connell studied was founded in 1596 by Father Parsons for English refugee priests. The same institution is referred to as having been the educational nursery of some of Queen Elizabeth's future opponents, and of some daring spirits who afterwards took part in the Gunpowder Plot. Murray states – I do not know on what authority – that Daniel O'Connell was trained here for the priesthood; but it is certain that just then the establishment was open to lay as well as to ecclesiastical students from England and Ireland. With the Revolution of 1793 the college was suppressed, only to start up, so to speak, like a phœnix from its ashes in 1802, under the name of 'Le College Communal', which became later on the Lyceum of Saint Omer. [. . .] The Lyceum still maintains no small amount of its former prestige, although the numbers of English and Irish students within its precincts is not so large as it was in the last century. The education curriculum is all that could be desired in the Lyceum, and the old Irish traditions of the institution are not forgotten.[. . .]

On the morning of the 18th August, 1792, O'Connell left Saint Omer, and on the evening of the same day reached the neighbouring town of Douai, where he was received as a student in the English College. Some writers fall into the error, by-the-by, of asserting that O'Connell was an alumnus of the Jesuit College of Douai; but I have it on the authority of the keeper of the municipal archives of Saint Omer that there was no such establishment in existence throughout that district in 1792 nor had there been any for a generation previous. The statement of this gentleman is furthermore confirmed by an eminent Douai clergyman, the Rev. Father Fossato O.S.B., who writes to me to the effect that it was at the English College of that town O'Connell prosecuted his studies. By a strange freak – or, shall I call it irony? – of fate this very college, under whose roof O'Connell may have conceived the elementary ideas of his moral force doctrine, is now, and has been for the past ninety-six years, a military barracks! In fact, the young Irishman had to leave it in the beginning of 1793, just as the French troops were making it their habitation and their home. The students' refectory is now a mess-room, and the former class halls are promenades for the soldiery in winter weather. [. . .] Admirers of O'Connell may moralise and say that the whirligig of Time does indeed bring about many and many a surprise. Some of the gorgeous palaces along the grand canal at Venice, where doges and senators met in luxurious wassail hundreds of years ago, are now depositories for hardware goods, or marts where the ring of the auctioneer's hammer is heard as he knocks down his twopenny-ha'penny gimcracks to the highest bidder! Even Imperial Caesar's dust may stop a bunghole!

O'Connell, in one of his letters from Douai, dated September 14th 1792, to his Derrynane uncle, says: 'The pension here is twenty-five guineas a year; but we get very small portions at dinner.' The young man's appetite was evidently dissatisfied with the microscopic viands that are usually served up on Continental tables. Variety of dishes may tickle the jaded palate; but the average Irishman, particularly if he be young, prefers, I dare say, a good substantial joint to all the tit-bits of the longest menu of the first of Parisian cooks. However that may be, young O'Connell was not quite happy in the College of Douai; and when the rumblings of the great Revolution grew more and more menacing, and when, owing to England's hostility to France, the lives of British subjects in the latter country were hardly worth a month's lease, Daniel took advantage of the opportunity offered him to write to his uncle, asking permission to return to England. Just as the letter containing this permission arrived, the College happened to be confiscated by the members of the municipality, who seized on all the plate and furniture of the establishment, and turned professors and students out of doors. O'Connell's violin was included in the general spoliation – a circumstance which may have contributed to the intense dislike for France and Frenchmen which was then, as it was afterwards, one of his most salient characteristics. The entire circumstances under which he quitted the country must have gone very far towards moulding his mind in what may now be looked on as a decidedly conservative cast. The excesses of the Revolutionary party made him shudder even at the very whisper of the word Revolution. So far as France was concerned, he was pleased to ignore the causes that led up to the popular upheaval; he would, doubtless, have considered his pity wasted on the beast of burden in the shape of man chained to the fields, or the pale, hollow-cheeked, desperate artisan earning starvation wages in the reeking attics of the big city; he was too essentially aristocratic, despite his democratic leanings, to denounce, as they should be denounced, the land-leeches who had lived and waxed fat in France on the life-blood of the people for centuries up to 1789. He only saw the devastating guillotine, and the sinister countenance of that arch-executioner, Robespierre, looming in the distance. The incipient virtues of the Revolution he had no consideration for; while he was blinded to everything save to its crimes and horrors.

This College was founded in 1569 by Cardinal Allen – firstly, for the education of English Catholic ecclesiastics, and later on for that of the English Catholic laity as well. Douai was chosen as the site of this establishment because it was hidden away in a quiet nook of land, and was at the same time within easy reach of British soil, and moreover, because it was the seat of a university which flourished up to 1793, when, like many other ecclesiastical institutions in France, it languished for some years till happier days came, and saw it revived and restored at Lille. Among the names of Douai students who suffered martyrdom for their championship of the Catholic faith in England I find those of Fathers Parsons, Campion and Cuthbert Mayne.

There were in the College in or about O'Connell's time several young men who made lasting reputation for themselves in after-life. Here it was where John Philip Kemble, one of England's leading tragedians, learned the elements of Rhetoric. Kemble at a very early age played various children roles in his father's theatre. Kemble senior was, however, in full harmony with the far from commendable spirit of the age in which he lived – a spirit which, though it relished comedy and tragedy on the stage with infinite gusto, refused, nevertheless, to tolerate comedians and tragedians in society off the stage. The father ambitioned a more 'respectable' career for his son, and with that view sent him to the Catholic seminary of Staffordshire, and from thence to the English College of Douai, where he studied for several years. No juvenile, however, can strut behind the footlights or taste the sweets of popular applause with anything like absolute impunity. Once the young eye fastens its gaze on an ocean of admiring faces, and once the young ear is charmed with the plaudits of pit and gallery, it is very hard for the stripling to escape from the fascination of stage life. He is in the position of one who having once trodden in dreams the smiling plains of some delightful Arcadia, grows sick of this jog-trot commonplace world of ours, and pines for the lustrous beauty which he had beheld through the magic lantern of his fancy. John Philip Kemble was one of these inveterate idealists. He accordingly threw up his class books at Douai at the age of nineteen, and returned to England, where he almost immediately afterwards became a favourite in Drury Lane, London, gaining the reputation of being a tragedian of consummate skill. His playing of the parts of Coriolanus, Cato and Macbeth crowned a fame that had been already solidly established. Kemble retired from the stage in 1817, and took up his residence at Lausanne, on the banks of Lake Leman, in Switzerland, where he lived the life of a recluse, and where he peacefully passed away in 1823. His brother Charles Kemble was also educated at Douai, and afterwards distinguished himself in the sphere of light, fantastic comedy.

Of quite different tastes and inclinations were two other Douai students of that epoch: one who became subsequently an eminent Catholic divine and antiquary, and who attained the rank of Vicar Apostolic of the Midland district in England, Dr Milner; and the Rev. John Lingard, also D.D., who penned the famous 'History of England'. Such are the names of a few of O'Connell's illustrious contemporaries in Douai. [. . .]

O'Connell left Douai on the 17th of January, 1793. A curious anecdote is told in connection with his departure from the shores of

France, which, I fancy, may be appropriately reproduced in these pages. Proceeding to Calais from Douai, he took shipping for Dover at the former town; and when the barque on which he was a passenger sailed outside the circle of French waters, the youth nonchalantly flung the tricolour cockade (which all residents of France were compelled to wear at the time) overboard, and looked as proud of the feat as if he had with a wave of his right hand restored the Bourbons to the throne of their ancestors! Was he not a typical nephew of the General in his devotion to the Lilies of France? It was on the occasion of the same voyage that he exchanged some hot words with John Sheares, the United Irishman from Cork, who had just returned from Paris, after having in the Place de la Concorde soaked his handkerchief in the blood of Louis XVI.

Douai itself is a town of some eighteen thousand inhabitants, situated pleasantly on the banks of the Scarpe, and is surrounded with fortifications now too old to be very redoubtable. Like Brussels, it is a straggling centre of population, containing far less souls to the square mile than Lille or Calais. Like the former, however, it is distinctively Flemish in its aspect. The carillon rings out its dulcet measures hour by hour from the magnificent belfry that looms in the market place above the Gothic Town Hall.

The denizens of Douai have, or used to have, an annual gala day in the early part of July, during which knights clad in antique armour flashed through the streets in all the glory of their war paint, escorted by patrician dames and damsels of the choicest brand, in the rere of whom filed a procession, composed of bloused farmers and rustic beauties tricked out in all kinds of gewgaws, and bearing a giant of osier standing thirty feet high in his sandals, arrayed in a stunning coat of mail, and accompanied by his tall and portly spouse and a family brood of proportionate width and girth worthy the dimensions of those darned fools of old who tried to scale the steps of starry Olympus in their warfare on the mighty Jove. Of the origin or history of this gigantic osier and his matrimonial incumbrances, I am as ignorant as I am of Volapuk. The whole procession was an elaborate enigma. Some of our sapient guide-books might contain a solution of the mystery; but I cannot dare to unravel it. The probabilities, however, are that this colossal osier must have been a hero in the flesh in the brave days of old, and as hero-worship is not yet an extinguished or even a decaying cult in any part of the civilised world, it would be the utmost folly to quarrel with the inhabitants of Douai if they keep up, though it be in harlequin style, one of those grand traditions of theirs which glorifies a great man.

Moreover, is it not well to be merry betimes? Surely we have not been born to pose through life in the attitudes of weeping statues, crying our eyes out perpetually over the cares and troubles, the pains and penalties of existence. I once knew a German who was never known to smile. He was rich in the world's wealth, and rich in the love of a fair young wife and a healthful progeny; and yet that man pined and drooped, and drooped and pined, and ultimately kicked the bucket in the full noon of manhood. And why? Simply because he could not enjoy his night's nap without reading beforehand 'The Sorrows of Werther'![2] If that man had taken proper exercise in the open air, and danced through a few carnivals every year, instead of mooning over the pages of maudlin woe and sentimentality, the desolate partner of his bosom would not now be on the lookout for a new lord and master. I do not see, therefore, why these people in Douai should not have their annual fling, and propitiate the god of pleasure after their own innocent fashion. Rabelais it was, I think, who said that a ripple of laughter on one's lips was infinitely better than a melancholy tear in one's eye. I must not, however, moralise further.

Returning to Douai, I may add that the mantle of the Irish and English scholars of past centuries has fallen on the shoulders of the monks of the Benedictine Order in that town. The English College, which these latter ecclesiastics have in charge, is called St Edmund's, and is the legitimate successor of the establishment in which O'Connell studied. Two of its most zealous professors are the Rev. Charles O'Neill, the worthy prior, and the Rev. P. W. Fassato. [. . .] St Edmund's, it may be observed, was originally established in Paris in 1611 by the monks of the English Benedictine Congregation. When the community of St George left Douai, and finally took up quarters at Downside, near Bath, St Edmund's was revived at Douai. The object of this institution is to educate youth principally for the priesthood, and so continue the work of the Irish, English and Scotch foundations established in the town throughout the sixteenth and seventeenth centuries. It is, I may add, exclusively occupied by English, Scotch and Irish students just now, and contains a debating club, in which Irish intellect holds its own very probably against all competition; while it affords special facilities for the study and the speaking of French. The juveniles who have a spark of the genius of a Gounod or a Wagner in them display its effulgence in the College Brass Band, from the repertory of which Irish music is by no means rigidly excluded. In addition to these attractions, the youth bitten with a mania for quill-driving will find a virgin field open to his exertions in the pages of a sparkling little magazine, 'The Edmundian', printed and published within the College walls. On the whole, St Edmund's of Douai is indeed one of the best institutions of its kind in France. [. . .]

Saint Malo, on the French coast, is another Irish landmark on the Continent; for it was in that little town where the somewhat erratic genius, the celebrated Father O'Leary, studied for the Church, and where he spent the first twenty-five years of his missionary career. This ecclesiastic played such an important part in the political life of Ireland towards the close of the last century that anything concerning him must have a distinctively historical value. Arthur O'Leary was born in the year 1729, of humble parents, in the parish of Fanlobbus, near Dunmanway, in the county of Cork. Like some others of the same name, he, too, claimed that royal – or, to put it more correctly, princely – ichor was flowing through his veins. [. . .] His lines thus fell on places where the rights and privileges of blue blood were as scrupulously respected as they were in the Vendée; and it is more than probable that it was amid these associations O'Leary became for the first time imbibed with those principles in which he was a consistent believer throughout his after life. O'Leary, the peasant lad, belonging as he did to the proscribed Church, and being brought up amid all the horrors of the Penal Days, soon discovered that he could not gratify at home his desire for knowledge. Being, moreover, inclined to a religious vocation, he left Ireland while he was still in his teens, and proceeded to the Capuchin Convent of Saint Malo, in Brittany, where he passed through the usual educational curriculum, and was duly promoted to holy orders. [. . .]

In the course of his career here an event occurred, the moral of which demonstrates very effectively his strange but fervid loyalty to the House of Hanover, and to the English Constitution at a time when his fellow-countrymen were groaning upon an odious and detestable tyranny, and owed as little devotion to the Court of St James as the serfs of the Sugar Plantations owed to their grinding taskmasters. It happened that throughout the seven years' war between the French and the English in the last century many British soldiers, most of whom were Irish and Catholic, were taken captive by the army of Louis, and were imprisoned at Saint Malo. The appointment of a chaplain to these men having become necessary, Father O'Leary was appointed to the post. While he held this position, the French Prime Minister, the Duc de Choiseul, sought to wean the Irish troops from their illogical allegiance to King George, and have them enrolled in the Irish Brigade, then fighting under the Bourbon flag. Wih this object Father O'Leary was approached, and was requested to use his influence with his fellow-countrymen in Saint Malo, and effect if possible their conversion; but the chaplain firmly declined the proposal. It is only just to Father O'Leary's memory to record here his own explanation of the attitude he assumed on this occasion: 'I thought it', he says, 'a crime to engage the King of England's soldiers and sailors in the service of a Catholic monarch against the Protestant Sovereign. I resisted the solicitations, and ran the risk of incurring the displeasure of a Minister of State and of losing my pension; but my conduct was approved of by the divines of the monastery to which I belonged.' The office of chaplain having ceased at the termination of the war in 1763, O'Leary was asked to accept the post of abbé in the French Court; but he declined this offer also under cover of the plea that he was 'a loyal subject of his British Majesty' and could on no account forswear his allegiance to that 'righteous sovereign.'

Unlike most of the Irish priests of his day, Father O'Leary was a devoted adherent of the Georges. If he had gone to Versailles, instead of returning to Cork, he would have been the right man in the right place as an 'abbé de la cour'; for he had all that suavity of manners and a grace and facility of expression, added to a dignified air and deportment, which were among the essential characteristics of the royal chaplains of those days.

Father O'Leary during his twenty-five years' sojourn in France used to spent his holidays in exploring the country on foot. He used to walk from the Convent of St Malo to the feet of the Pryenees, or promenade all the way from the gates of Paris to the banks of the Rhine backwards and forwards within a month. Mark Twain's tramp abroad was petty and insignificant compared with that of Father Arthur.

The rev. gentleman had a curious adventure while he was on a visit to a brother clergyman in Boulogne-sur-Mer. He was strolling one evening along the quays, when he happened to encounter a large crowd of people forming a circle around a bear and his keeper. Father Arthur, piqued by curiosity, edged his way into the forefront in order to witness the performances of this wonderful animal, whose fame for several days previously had gone the rounds of all Boulogne, for this was no ordinary bear. He was, in fact, a trained and disciplined beast; for he could mark with his paw on the sand the hour of the clock; he could nod to the gentlemen, and make an Oriental salaam to the ladies with a grace and affability quite foreign to members of his grizzly order. On the occasion in question the keeper, armed with a long steel-pointed pole, kept the beast at his work, and every five minutes pocketed the coins of admiring spectators. The bear, having been hard-pressed all day, eventually grew tired of the performance, and showed a disposition to sulk, when the keeper gave him two or three sharp pricks with the goad, whereupon the animal cursed and shouted in a language the meaning of which was understood by none present except Father O'Leary himself, who immediately exclaimed – 'Cianos tha'n thu, a Phadring?' ('How do you do, Pat?'). 'Slán, go raimh math agut!' ('Pretty well, thank you!'), rejoined the bear. Father O'Leary lost no time in summoning the Mayor of Boulogne to the scene and explaining the situation to that official, who discovered that some blackguard fishermen had actually sewed up a poor Irishman in a bear's skin, and were making a pile of money by exhibiting the extraordinary animal. The skin was immediately ripped open, and after some difficulty Pat stepped forth in Adam's original costume, to the astonishment of the men, and to the utter confusion of the women, who turned and fled in the wildest dismay. According to Sir Jonah Barrington, the bear afterwards told O'Leary that he was very well fed and did not care much about the inconvenience of the clothing, only they worked him too hard. The fishermen, he said, found him at sea on a hen-coop, which had saved him from going to the bottom with a ship in which he had a little venture of dried cod from Dungarvan, and which was bound from Dungarvan to Bilboa. He could not speak a word of any language except Irish, and was delighted to find a fellow-countryman to whom he could explain his grievances. When Father Arthur subsequently returned to Ireland this anecdote was one of many others with which he would set his friends into roars of laughter at convivial tables. [. . .]

O'Leary was residing in London when the Revolution burst over France. From the very inception of the Revolutionary movement the rev. father was, of course, bitterly but consistently opposed to it. He had been a French priest of the old regime for twenty-five years. The principles he imbibed in the wilds of West Cork were fortified tenfold on the coast of Saint Malo, where the veneration for royalty prevails among nearly all classes even to the present day. The polished manners of the choice Bourbon nobility, in whose midst he had moved, left their impress on him; and his devotion to the ancient nobility – naturally enough – prompted him to weep over their fall, or denounce in burning language what he considered to be their outrageous spoilation. It is no wonder, therefore, that in a sermon preached by him in St Patrick's Chapel in London he should have used the following language in alluding to the leaders of the French democracy:

> By decree the French declare that they are willing to give assistance to all who wish to procure liberty. By this decree the desperate, the licentious, the dissolute of all nations, who would wish the overthrow of their respective countries in order to enrich themselves with the spoils of the peaceable and the virtuous, were sure to find allies and confederates.

Language somewhat similar to this has, if I mistake not, been applied to the Irish democracy of modern days by men who would have it lie tame and submissive for ever, in order that their own cellars may continue to be provided with the choicest wines, and their larders may never fail of provisions. The 'licentious' and the 'dissolute' of all nations are not found among the people. They are to be met with among the peers and paladines of long descent, and the Shylock gentry who pamper themselves on the spoils wrung from the horny hands of labour. The idle dudes, who form the bulk of the tinselled nobility, possess a goodly portion of swag, to which they have as little right as any average footpad who knocks down a belated wayfarer and relieves him of his watch. The shibboleths of 'robbery' and 'spoliation' flung in the teeth of the people's champions by these kid-gloved moralists sound as awkwardly as a sermon on the beauty and efficacy of virtue from the lips of Satan. As Mephistopheles in *Faust* wisely remarked, 'that which you call the "better blood" makes the worst person; and as for the "best", the devil himself would blush for them!'

Father O'Leary was such a staunch champion of the British government under the peculiar circumstances of the time that his orthodoxy became suspected in Ireland, and among the other stories circulated regarding him was one to the effect that, like Lord Dunboyne, he too meditated giving up the priesthood in order to become a benedict. John Butler, the twelth Lord Dunboyne, had been for twenty-three years the Catholic Bishop of Cork, and was the first instance on record, with the exception of Archbishop Browne of Dublin, of a Catholic prelate changing his religion. If Lord Dunboyne had not inherited the family title and estate, the probabilities are that he would have remained faithful to his clerical vows to the end. At a very advanced age, however, he was raised to the peerage by the death of his nephew, Pierce Edmund Butler; and, professing a desire to perpetuate his lineage, he begged of the Holy See to permit him to marry. The Holy See, of course, refused to accord him any such dispensation, but the prelate was nevertheless determined to carry out his own wishes irrespective of the opposition of the Pope and the Propaganda. He shortly afterwards espoused a beautiful girl of some seventeen summers, who was a relative of his own, and the daughter of Theobald Butler, of Wilford, in the county of Tipperary. There was no issue of this unhappy marriage; and the aged prelate passed away some years subsequently, after having made on his dying bed as ample a reparation as possible for his unfortunate apostacy. At the time of Lord Dunboyne's marriage Father O'Leary, who, as I have said, was also accused of meditating a similar step, thus replied to his calumniators –

> I do not consider Lord Dunboyne as a model whom I should copy. With his silver locks, and at an age when persons who had devoted themselves to the services of the altar in their early days, should, like Emperor Charles V, rather think of their coffins rather than of the nuptial ring, that prelate married a young woman. Whether the glowing love of truth or Hymen's torch induced him to change the Roman Pontifical for the Book of Common Prayer, and the psalms he and I often sang together for a bridal hymn, his own conscience is the most competent to judge or determine . . . Your correspondent may rest assured that I am not one of the trio mentioned in his letter.

To the credit of the Irish Catholic Church be it said that the apostates in its hierarchy and priesthood could be easily counted on one's fingers. No Catholic ecclesiastics all the world over have been as pure, as steadfast, or as devoted in their faith as the Irish. The remaining two apostates referred to in the trio were Dean Kirwan, Bishop of Ardagh, and Dr Thomas Lewis O'Beirne, who afterwards became Protestant Bishop of Meath. Dean Kirwan was educated at Louvain; while O'Beirne passed through his educational course in various French colleges, and finally at St Omer's. Returning to the latter establishment from his holidays in Ireland, he happened to be thrown into the society of two travellers in the inn of an English country village; and having spent an entertaining evening in their company he was agreeably surprised on the following morning when he discovered that his companions were none other than Charles Fox and the Duke of Portland,[3] both of whom invited him to their London residences and promised him their patronage. O'Beirne had all the polish and elegance of manners that characterised Irish ecclesiastics of that day who were educated on the Continent, and soon became such a prominent figure and general favourite in the gilded salons of the British capital that he soon abandoned the idea of further prosecuting his studies for the Church, and embraced the Anglican faith. Having no small share of literary attainments, he acted for some time in the capacity of secretary of the Duke of Portland, and in his leisure moments translated two dramas from the French, and was assisted in their adaptation for the stage by the Duchess of Devonshire; but the productions, when played behind the footlights, proved to be abject failures. On Lord Fitzwilliam's appointment to the Irish Viceroyalty, O'Beirne, who in the meantime had entered Holy Orders, accompanied him as chaplain and private secretary, and was shortly afterwards rewarded for his services by the opulent Bishopric of Meath, valued at £8,000 a year. He held this post up to his death; and it was a strange and curious coincidence that he should have been the Protestant prelate of a diocese in which at the same time his brother, who was also educated at St Omer's, was discharging the functions of a Catholic parish priest.

Of Father O'Leary little more remains to be told. His devotion to the House of Hanover brought him the reward of a Government pension. On this ticklish subject we have the authority of a well-informed correspondent of O'Leary's biographer, the late learned Father Buckley, of Cork, who writes as follows on the part which the Friar took by the advice of Pitt in his union of the Irish Parliament with the Imperial:

> Pitt promised the emancipation of Catholics and the repeal of the Penal Laws if he (O'Leary) would acquiesce. He did; and so silence

> was deemed consent. Pitt obtained the Union, then resigned his office, and, tricky enough, said he could not keep his promise. The memory of the disaster weighed upon his mind, so that, dying, he often exclaimed – 'Alas! I have betrayed my poor country!'

Like other Irishmen, O'Leary was hoodwinked by false promises and wheedled by glozing bunkum. The treaty stone of Limerick had for him no damning souvenirs of violated oaths and undisguised treachery. Posterity in Ireland may forgive him for his credulity; but his acceptance of hush money cannot under any circumstances be condoned – particularly when it is known that his influence was so great that had he opposed the Union it is problematical that that ill-fated measure could have been carried out by Pitt and Castlereagh.

A few months before the end came, Father O'Leary, accompanied by a medical friend, crossed the Channel to France in search of health. He was, it seems, sorely shocked by the contrast which the country presented with its condition in the experience of his youth and early manhood. The whole aspect of society had undergone a radical change. Democracy, it appears, ruled the roast to such an extent that the Friar, while he was on one occasion visiting the charred ruins of a chateau in Brittany, exclaimed – 'Alas! there is not now one gentleman in the entire of France.' He returned to London disgusted and afflicted in spirit with what he had seen, and died in that city on the 8th of January, 1802. His remains lie interred in the churchyard of St Pancras, in that city, while a monument bearing an appropriate inscription and erected to his memory may still be seen in St Patrick's Chapel.

Saint Malo, the scene of Father O'Leary's missionary labours for a quarter of a century, contains some ten thousand inhabitants, and is a favourite resort of fishermen. A brisk trade is being carried on here in cordage and fishing nets, which are manufactured with much skill and taste. Saint Malo has, however, seen better days. One hundred years ago it was a thriving centre of population, although its wealth, speaking generally, was not acquired by very scrupulous means. In the old times, when smuggling between Saint Malo and several English ports was carried on in spanking style, the citizens were enabled to give handsome dowries to their daughters. Now, alas! many of the fair ones have to depend on their faces for a fortune, and seldom or never succeed in winning the hands of men who earn respectable incomes; for here, as well as elsewhere throughout France, portionless girls, no matter how well reared or educated they may be, must either resign themselves to the cheerless lot of elderly maidenhood or else become the wives of labourers. The sailors of Saint Malo are the best in France. The poet Jean Richepin,[4] who lived among them for several years, says that their chests are of cast iron and their sinews are of oak! In past years, it may be remembered they manned scores of privateers, and pirated along the English coast. The English in turn retorted by treating Saint Malo to periodical attentions of shell and shot. Traditions of those days still linger around the hearthsides of the old town, where tales are told of the brave Gallic tar who scuttled many a Carthaginian brig and peppered the white hills of Dover. [. . .]

The Irish traveller on the continent would do well to visit Brittany; for there, he might almost say, he will find himself among his own. It seems even as if the climate had caught the infection of the race, for on the Breton as on the Irish coast there is a rather decided moisture in the atmosphere unknown in other parts of France, and rains are by no means rare. I have spent some very pleasant weeks in the province and found the people as genial, as good natured and as warm-hearted as if they were 'kindly Irish of the Irish, neither Saxon nor Italian', despite the fact that that melancholy ocean created by the late Lord Beaconsfield[5] out of his own inner consciousness pours its eternal wailings into their ears. Brothers of the Irish, in that they are Celts, they are a brave and hospitable people. Travelling among them I was surprised to find what I may be permitted to call duplicates of what I had seen years before in Ireland: the hoary cromleach, the ruins of the Druid's altar, and the rings where belts of fire blazed in the long ago to glorify the Sun. Bal and Astarte were worshipped here as they were amid the hills of Innisfail. The great primeval forests, where the Breton Pagan assembled, and where, in the whisperings of the breeze through the oak tree and chestnut, they fancied they heard the accents of an unknown divinity, still stud the province. In the humble homesteads beside the crackling fire vanithees tell tales that are told in Ireland even to-day around the welcome turf in the long winter evenings; tales of fairy mythology, in which changelings, fairy men and fairy women, the merrow maiden and the merrow man, the Leanhaun Shee and the Leprechaun, wizard knights and Balors of the Evil Eye, figure as shadowy characters; tales of apparitions and fetches of warriors like Finn of Fomosian chiefs, and tales of deeds of mighty prowess which call back to the mind sweet, innocent memories of the days of our prattling childhood. The Bretons are, like their forefathers, a vividly imaginative race. They see gorgeous palaces in the piles of roseate clouds that camp above the setting sun in a gorgeous summer's evening. Some of them still believe they hear the songs of mermaids by the seashore in the moonlit nights. They cherish with love and fondness all their old legends and traditions, and to such an extent have they merged their individuality in that of the nation at large that the traveller who has seen the rest of France, and who penetrates into this province for the first time, will ask himself has he crossed any frontier, and looks in vain for custom-house officers to check his baggage. To their credit be it said, they speak the tongue of their ancestors in all the country districts, as well as, partially though it be, in such towns as Rennes and Nantes.

A press colleague of mine, Baron Platel, the 'Ignotus' of the *Figaro*,[6] told me on one occasion during my residence in Paris a curious anecdote dealing with the Bretons and the Irish. The Baron was born and reared in a country-house by the Breton sea, and at various times during his boyhood he had opportunities of meeting Irish sailors, who landed at a neighbouring port. 'I knew', he said, 'by their dress and by their accent that they were foreigners, for I could swear they were neither Bretons nor French. Well, I saw the Breton sailors shake their hands, and I heard them converse together in Gaelic. Off and on, it is true, they failed to comprehend each other's meaning, but on the whole they understood each other with facility. On the first occasion I was so much piqued by curiosity at this extraordinary scene that I asked a bluff old Breton captain who the foreigners were. 'Sacre! Sacre!', muttered the veteran sea-dog between his teeth, 'they are not foreigners to us – they are Irish. Their language and ours is almost the same!'

Today in Paris the Breton colony keeps up its individuality. Its members are represented in the press by the 'Revue Celtique' and they have their monthly Celtic dinners, at which the deputies and senators, the essayists and novelists, the pressmen and poets, the dramatists and painters of Brittany dwell in song and story over the glories, the traditions, the history and the beauty of that brave old Celtic land from whence they came with light hearts to face the difficulties of life in the streets and on the boulevards of the capital.

A BIRD'S EYE VIEW OF PARIS

A little national vanity is not only not a vice in a people, but it may even be considered a virtue, if indulged in or practised within reasonable limits. It is often the incentive to mighty deeds, the creator of sublime feelings and the very essence of that self-respect without which a nation, like the individual, would be a base and contemptible factor in the world's social economy. The Muscovite can be as proud of his steppes and the Laplander of his snows as the Spaniard is of his olive groves and the Roman of the ruins of his Forum. True enough, this sentiment of national vanity may be carried to ridiculous excesses and become under certain circumstances a great absurdity.

The Frenchman had up to the fall of the Second Empire an exaggerated national vanity which was near becoming his ruin. The disaster of Sedan, the ignominious capitulation of Metz, and the wholesale defeat of his battalions by the Teuton invaders, opened his eyes to the truth and chastened him to a very considerable extent indeed. The love of the Frenchman for France, is, however, cold enough when compared with the love of the Parisian for Paris.

Victor Hugo called the gay capital the brain of France and the heart of the world's fashion and amusement. His city is in the eyes of the average Parisian the queen of all cities, as beauteous as Cleopatra and as prodigal of her favours; the sanctuary of intellect, and the shrine of refinement. He may go off to the seaside for a few weeks every summer; he may visit the casinos of Dieppe and Trouville, or pitch his tent in Ostend; but the hotels in which he frequents must be conducted by Parisians; he must be served at table by Parisian waiters, and the theatricals he attends must be carried on by Parisian artistes. Even then, he falls a victim to the nostalgy of the boulevards; and it is with a light heart he returns to that happy hunting-ground of his which lies between the Madeleine and the Bastille. Like most of his newspapers, he takes only a languid interest in any events occurring outside the fortifications. He would yawn over the details of a big fire in America; but his heart would beat and his eyes would glisten over a reporter's interview with Woerth, the ladies' tailor, in the Rue de la Paix. The doings and opinions of Paulus, the music-hall singer, are realised by him with infinite gusto; while a Presidential election in the States or a nihilist outbreak in Russia are flat, stale, and unprofitable themes, to which he is as indifferent as he is to the financial condition of the Republic of Chili. In fact an item of news recording how Sarah Bernhardt sprained her ankle, or gravely announcing that the 'brave general'[7] did not partake of the morning's café-au-lait with his usual appetite, would pique his curiosity more than the death of an Emperor or a Ministerial crisis in England. Under these circumstances it is no wonder that he should display a profound ignorance of foreign affairs. He is so engrossed with the business of his own city that he has neither the time nor the taste to occupy himself with that of the world in general.

Yet Paris is, perhaps, the most cosmopolitan of cities. Representatives of all semi-civilised races, and of mostly all civilised ones, rub up their skirts against each other on the boulevards. Here the Russian Prince sips his perfumed wines in the Jockey Club, while his wife and daughters, lolling in an open easy carriage and smoking dainty Turkish cigarettes, drive up the Champs Elysées, and around the lake in the Bois de Boulogne, where the wealth and fashion of Paris, the 'monde' and the 'demi-monde', fair circus riders and wrinkled dowager-duchesses, spick-and-span dudes and elegant marchionesses, gaudily attired adventuresses and bankers who act as cavaliers, nobles and swindlers, the 'crème de la crème' of Bourbon knightships, and the rag-tag and bob-tail of roguery, in broadcloth and jewellery, congregate in all their tinsel finery to admire and be admired, to smirk and bow, and bandy oily platitudes to each other in a Babel of tongues.

In Paris one may enter a café the proprietor of which is a son of the Alps, and quaff 'the little white wine of the Pays de Vaud', a beverage which I never could take without making the wryest of faces, but which nevertheless goes down the average Swiss throat with the mellow sweetness of the honey of Hymettus. Elsewhere one may betake himself to a Strasbourg beer-ship, where the ale of the Rhine or the sparkling Bavarian liquid is most patronised by

Austrians and Germans; and should you go up the Rue Royale, and peep in at the Irish-American Bar, you will, if you are an Irishman, find yourself among your own, where the smiling face of a Connaughtman beams its welcome upon you from behind the counter, and where Hibernians from all the four provinces, with the patriotic aim of supporting and encouraging home manufacture take an odd glass of Guinness or John Jameson. Quite close in the same street, as well as in the streets in the immediate vicinity, are English establishments where the 'Arries, who belong chiefly to the better confraternity, will tickle your ears with the choicest slang, while quaffing beakers of Bass or sipping thimble-full glasses of Old Tom. Lower down along the boulevards are Spanish and Italian, Greek and Hungarian houses, where the dusky children of the South, passionate and fiery as the sun of their native lands, chatter and gesticulate in a manner that would astonish the cooler and unsophisticated native of northern climes.

To the pleasure seeker or the epicurean Paris is a bewitching fairyland. Should he be theatrically inclined, he has no less than sixty theatres to choose from, one dozen at least of which are exceedingly well-appointed in decoration as well as in the superior talents of the troupes; the Comédie Française,[8] where Racine and Molière among the ancient, and Sardou[9] and Dumas[10] among the moderns, delight and enthral the audience; the Odeon, where François Coppée holds his own, and wins the applause of the students; the Grand Opera, where Verdi and Gounod sit, so to speak, enthroned; the 'Théâtre Libre', where the young talents of France, the budding playwrights and comedians of the land, conceive daring and original thoughts, or assume daring and original characters; the tragic and diaphanous Sarah,[11] winsome Judic,[12] Coquelin the elder,[13] clad in the flowing robes and crowned with the orthodox peruke of one of the doctors of Molière, Coquelin the younger, the manipulator-in-chief of the monologue, and hosts of others. The more or less admired of the

Parisian population invariably command the admiration of the foreigner as well.

In the warm summer evenings, when most of the theatres are closed for the annual holiday, and those that remain open are literal furnaces, the visitor can call in at one of the four or five open-air music-halls in the Champs Elysées and enjoy himself under the shadow of the trees over his coffee, while listening to the songs and beholding the antics of the third-class actors and actresses on stage. The unwary tourist is, however, generally always 'taken in' during his first visit to one of these establishments. Over the rustic gateway his eye catches a signboard with the alluring inscription, 'Entrée Libre', or entrance free. He goes in unsuspectingly, as does a fly into the spider's parlour, and takes his seat in an arm-chair close to the stage. Shortly afterwards he calls for a cup of coffee or a glass of beer, and having taken off the beverage, he asks the price, and is amazed to be told that the insignificant drink costs two francs and a half. So you see that 'Entrance Free' is a little bit of word-jugglery to deceive the credulous. Many are caught by this seductive signboard. I was hardly a week in Paris when I was pinned and fleeced – financially, of course – within its precincts. The burnt child dreads the fire with far less intensity than I dreaded that same music-hall for years afterwards throughout those salad days of youth, when the purse was light and the Fates were unpropitious. One evening, however, accompanied by a fellow-countryman, I was passing up the 'Heavenly Fields',[14] when a fellow suspiciously resembling one of these lank, seedy, bullet-headed Bohemians, who may be found loafing all day long around the doors of third-rate Continental playhouses, approached me, and asked if we would not come into the music-hall – a glass of beer being only sixpence apiece on that particular evening. My comrade and I, baited by this rosy-coloured tariff, accepted the stranger's proposal; and we soon found ourselves in the midst of as motley a group of poor devils as ever I gazed on, seated at the end of the garden facing the stage, and comprising in all some half-dozen oddities, ill-kempt, ill-clad starvelings, whose hollow cheeks and over-lustrous eyes told of want and hunger, but whose long flowing locks were proof enough that they belonged to that vast array of artistes who throng the attics and stablelofts of Paris. And apropos of the word 'artiste', I may be allowed to mention here that it is a more comprehensive term on the banks of the Seine than it is on the banks of the Liffey. The editor of a newspaper is an 'artiste', and so is his office-boy; for they both belong to the glorious guild of journalism, which is ranked as one of the fine arts abroad. The operatic star of the period is an 'artiste', and so is her clever little maid who looks after her lady's bodice, manipulates her tresses, and tricks her out in gewgaws of paste-jewellery for the evening's performance. The hall porter of a theatre is an 'artiste'. Returning to my story, I have to add that when the 'prima donna' of the establishment, a painted, powdered piece of elderly goods, tripped it lightly over the stage and bowed to the audience, the stranger, who appeared to be the chief of our group, addressing us in bated whisper, said 'now my friends, when I give you the signal to clap, clap; and when I tell you to be mum, be mum!' The features of my fellow Irishman, usually very ruddy indeed, grew sickly pale at this revelation. He looked, as Mark Twain would put it, tolerably unwell; but as there was no decent escape from the position in which we found ourselves, we burst out laughing at the idea that we had just become a pair of improvised clappers, members of the confraternity of the 'claque'; so we bore up bravely with our lot for the remainder of the evening, and grinned. On retiring to rest at midnight, we found the palms of our hands as purple as the robes of kings!

Having said so much of the Parisian, my fair readers may ask if I have nothing to say of the 'Parisienne'. Well, the more interesting portion of humanity is practically the same all the world over – be its representative the snow-skinned maid of the North, or the dusky quadroon of the South. Nigger women alone must take a back seat in the gallery; yet I dare say there are nigger men who consider these mates of theirs handsome, for there are peculiar people about who can see a thing of beauty in the brow of Egypt. The Parisienne is, generally speaking, a willowy lady, whose features, though somewhat pale, incline to a mild olive tint; whose hands and feet are coquettishly small, and whose toilette is always in harmony with the latest vogue of fashion. She of all others knows the practical art of dress to perfection. Whether it be the 'grande dame' of the Faubourg, in whose Venetian laces is enshrined much of the balm of Araby, or the winsome little shop-girl with the laughing eyes and the slightly *retroussé* nose, the Parisienne may well bear off the cake for taste and distinction of manners. Her gait is poetically graceful. Unlike some awkward English girls, who usually take elephantine strides while 'doing' the boulevards, she barely puts one foot before the other in a promenade, and nevertheless glides briskly along like a swan or a dream of walking music. In society she is a siren of sirens in polish of deportment, although in many cases she has little of the serpent in her frank, generous nature. Her conversation is sparkling and witty – that is to say, if she be privileged to take part in a conversation; for if she be a spinster, she must curb her tongue and nurse its undeveloped powers until she can exercise it on the husband who is selected for her. Married ladies and widows, however, have no such muzzles on their fair lips; and they talk and talk of everything under the sun, from the latest ministerial crisis to the cut of the latest bonnet, discussing as they go on the last play written by Dumas or the last novel penned by Daudet, the best costumes of the Diva Bernhardt, and the tenderest sonnets of the poet Coppée, never dealing with any subject profoundly, but touching it on the surface with a native delicacy peculiarly their own.

I am not, however, in the mood to pile virtue after virtue on the pretty head of the Parisienne. All over Europe, and across the big fish pond may, perhaps, be found the same idyllic woman – that sweet seraphic creature who has all of the angel in her, save the wings; and I do not know that the daughters of Paris can legitimately presume to possess a monopoly of the perfections of the sex. [. . .]

Politeness, like other arts, fine and superfine, is liable at times to be abused. The juvenile who would stand for half an hour of a wild March day in the streets of Paris with head uncovered while conversing with a lady, just to show his callow enthusiasm for the sex, and who bows off and on before the beauty like a stage courtier, may be the very essence of good breeding; but considering that his gallantry may cost him a cold, and a cold may cost him his life, it would not be going too far to say that he is a consummate idiot. [. . .]

THE IRISH IN PARIS BEFORE 1848

One of the earliest Irish exiles in Paris was St Fiachra. The exact time in which this holy man was prosecuting his missionary labours on the banks of the Seine is not known nor can it be ascertained. It is, however, certain that it must have been somewhere near the close of the fifth century. Many of my readers will, I daresay, be astonished to learn that Fiachra, the Irishman, was the patron saint of the cabbies of Paris. At an age when scepticism was unknown, and long before Diderot and Voltaire produced their Encyclopedia, St Fiachra had his shrine, and was duly honoured by the Jehus of the big city. Now the veneration for the Saint is not so marked, but it is nevertheless profound. The 'cochers', who call their vehicles 'fiacres', in honour of the Irish missionary, meet here and there in groups on the Saint's day, and celebrate his anniversary as best they can. [. . .]

The Irishman who visits the Latin Quarter of Paris, and who catches a glimpse of the far-famed Sorbonne, will inevitably be reminded of Duns Scotus, although, of course, the building in which that eminent theologian pontificated has long since ceased to exist. The name of the Sorbonne itself will, however, remain imperishably connected with that of the celebrated Duns.

Cities, we are told, contended for the honour of claiming Homer as one of their denizens, although while Homer lived they gave him a stone when he asked for bread. Nations quarrel over the glory of having given birth to Scotus. Englishmen assert that the famous divine belonged to their own nationality; Scotchmen would have us believe that he was a son of the land o' cakes; while Irishmen stoutly protest that he was a true-born Milesian. One eminent authority says that he was a native of Dunse, in Berwickshire, and goes the length of stating that the ruins of the old homestead in which he first saw the light can still be pointed out in that locality! According to the Irish version of his life, Duns Scotus was born at Thalhmon, or Taghmon, in the present county of Wexford, although there are some who would give Downpatrick credit for having been his birthplace. Nearly all versions agree on the point that he was educated in England, and was for some time a professor in one of the learned institutions of that country. He proceeded from thence to Paris, and defended in the Sorbonne, before the theological magnates of that day, in a public thesis, the Immaculate Conception of Mary. This disputation continued for over a week, in the course of which Scotus demolished no less than 2,000 objections to his theory, and came triumphantly out of the ordeal. The worth and solidity of his arguments made a lasting impression on the theology of the Catholic Church – so much so, in fact, that the doctrine he propounded towards the close of the thirteenth century was solemnly proclaimed a dogma of the Catholic community in the nineteenth.

His success was so great that he was immediately nominated professor of the university, and from his curule chair by the Seine he as ardently defended his own theological opinions as he combatted those of the Thomists. A writer who assisted at his lectures in the

Sorbonne says that he 'resolved the knottiest syllogisms of his adversaries as Samson did the bands of Dalilah' – the result being that he converted the leading lights of the university and its thousand of students to this own theories. His cheese-paring logical discrimination eventually won him the title of the 'subtle doctor'. In 1318 he was sent to Cologne to found a university, and on reaching that city he was met by the inhabitants and carried on their shoulders to the cathedral. His name and fame spread all over Europe, and the schools applauded him as the most learned of professors. After having spent several years in the new university Duns Scotus died in a rather strange manner. Attacked one day with a stroke of apoplexy, he was buried alive, and, when later on his coffin was opened, the analysts who saw his remains stated their conviction that he must have knocked out his brains against the lid. A facetious chronicler of the day said that he well deserved the title of 'subtle', his subtlety having commenced before his birth, for no one has yet been able to track him to his first appearance in our world, and having ended in the bosom of mother earth, where he would not give his fellow men the satisfaction of knowing at what precise moment he passed away. Some centuries afterwards Luke Wadding collected and published in several volumes the writings of this illustrious scholar.

Many Irishmen received their educational training within the walls of the Sorbonne. Throughout the Penal Days the number of Hibernian students was particularly large. Shortly after Duns Scotus departed from Paris, Thomas Palmer, usually styled Thomas Hibernicus, became a Fellow of the University, and subsequently a professor of theology. One of the rectors of the University was Michael Moore, a native of Bridge Street, Dublin, who rose to that high rank by the sheer force of talent and merit. Michael Moore having received a good classical education at home, repaired to France, where he commenced his ecclesiastical studies in the Irish College of Nantes. He subsequently proceeded to Paris, where he concluded his education course, and, having returned to Ireland, was in due course of time ordained a priest by Luke Wadding, Bishop of Ferns. His zeal and ability proved to be so remarkable that he was soon promoted to the position of Prebendary of Tymothan and Vicar-General of Dublin. Owing, however, to the fact that it was practically impossible for him, in fact of the religious persecution that was raging all around, to fulfil his priestly functions in the capital, he was compelled to exile himself once more, and settled down in Paris, where he forced the doors of the most eclectic social salons, held converse with the titled magnates and literary men of the day, and won the esteem and friendship of Cardinal Noailles,[15] that great ecclesiastic of whom it is written that 'he loved what was good and did it'. His Eminence encouraged the Irish priest in his career, and viewed with the utmost satisfaction his appointment to the chair of Greek, Hebrew, and Philosophy in the Sorbonne, and his subsequent elevation to the presidency of the College of Navarre and rectorship of the University of Paris. Thus it happened that the two greatest universities of the Middle Ages were at one time governed by Irishmen – Louvain by Dr Stapleton of Tipperary, and the Sorbonne by Dr Moore of Dublin. It may be added that Pope Innocent XII was so well pleased with Dr Moore's rectorship that he made a donation of two thousand crowns a year to the institution. His Holiness Clement XI esteemed Moore so highly that he placed one of his nephews under his tuition. Though honours of which any man might legitimately feel proud were being showered upon him in the land of his adoption, his heart remained unalterably attached to the land of his birth. He was most assiduous in looking after the welfare of the Irish students in Paris. After many years spent in useful labours the venerable scholar died in the College of Navarre on the 22nd of August, 1726, and his remains were interred in the chapel of the old Irish College, an establishment to which he bequeathed his valuable library. Dr Moore was not only a distinguished professor, but also an erudite and successful author, several of his works written in Latin and French being still treasured in ecclesiastical seminaries.

Another prominent Irish 'alumnus' of the Sorbonne was Cornelius Nary, of the county of Kildare. [. . .] Among the other distinguished alumni of Paris may be mentioned Thomas Messingham the author of a 'Garland of Irish Saints'; John Macgeoghegan, who wrote a 'History of Ireland', which John Mitchel has brought down to our own day; Malachi O'Queely, the friend of John Colgan, and author of a learned dissertation on the islands of Arran; Geoffrey Keating and Sylvester O'Halloran, the celebrated historians; Neil O'Glacan, first among physicians; and Dr William Coppinger, the apostle of asceticism.

The Sorbonne is situated quite close to the Cluny Museum, off the Boulevard St Michel, and was originally founded for sixteen poor students by the Chevalier Robert de Sorbonne, from whom it took its name. Small at first, it gradually assumed larger and larger proportions, till it became the standard school for theology and canon law, while the disputations that took place within its walls swayed to a certain extent the Church in France, and gave it that Gallican tinge which only wholly disappeared a short time ago. The existing edifice was built by Cardinal Richelieu; but since 1853 modern wings have been added, and very little of the original remains. For several hundred years it was exclusively the seat of philosophy and theology. Since the Revolution, however, the sciences and letters have been added to its programme, three of the five faculties of the Academy of Paris being in the hands of its directing committee. The University contains very spacious lecture and anatomy halls, a splendid museum of national history, and a library of some 100,000 volumes. The church attached to the University is visited by the tourist chiefly for the purpose of seeing the tomb where the illustrious Richelieu sleeps his last sleep. It may be interesting to know, in conclusion, that there are still Irish associations clustering around the Sorbonne. In the roll of its students one meets Irish names belonging either to the descendants of the old Irish Brigade, Irish-Americans, or natives of Ireland who are preparing for the law, medicine or engineering. Some eminent Irish professional men in Paris took out their degrees in the establishment; and although, of course, it has lost, through the force of competition, much of its early pomp and eclat, the examinations within its precincts are severe enough, and qualification for a degree is extremely difficult.

Not very far from the Sorbonne the traveller happens on the Conciergerie and the Place de Grève, associated with the memory of an Irishman, Count Lally Tollendal, one of the heroes of Fontenoy.[16] It was in the Conciergerie where Lally spent the last weeks of his life, and it was in the Place de Grève where he was executed. Never was there a more atrocious stigma on the escutcheon of any government than such an execution. Lally had won undying glory at Fontenoy; he had spent his youth and manhood in the service of France, not only in Europe but in the West Indies, and France rewarded the soldier by delivering him up to the executioner's axe. [. . .] The Place de Grève, where this judicial murder of an illustrious Irishman took place, was the large square in front of the old Hotel de Ville. From time immemorial executions were the order of the day on that fatal spot. It was here, too, that the first victims of the Revolutionary terror were swung up to lamp irons and hurled into eternity. Since the demolition of the old houses on its northern and western sides, nothing now, however, remains of the Place de Grève save its site.

St Germain, one of the suburbs of Paris, was for many years the home of illustrious Irish exiles, for here in the Palace of the Bourbons, James II, after the disaster of the Boyne, held his court, and was surrounded on state occasions by many of the veterans who fought his battles in Ireland, and who clung to him even more closely in the evening of his life, when there was no longer any serious hope of re-establishing the Stuart dynasty. The Dillons and McCarthys, the O'Neills and the O'Donnells were among James's cavaliers in St Germain; and here in the court balls officers of the Irish Brigade out for a holiday would be seen tripping through the minuet with the winsome daughters of France. In these gilded halls, under the subdued light of waxen tapers ensconced in the candelabra overhead, 'eyes looked love to eyes that spoke again', and matrimonial alliances were settled whereby many a French lass exchanged her Gallic name for one bearing the stamp of an 'O' or 'Mac'. This palace was, however, no Capuan retreat for Ireland's exiled officers. The aged amongst them resided here continuously; but those in active service could only visit it once or twice during the year, save in time of peace or public tranquillity.

St Germain can be reached from the St Lazare Station, and is situated some fourteen miles from Paris, on the left bank of the Seine. Standing on an eminence it commands a very fine view of the city. The chateau so intimately associated with Irish souvenirs can still be visited by the tourist, who will find himself deeply interested while exploring the wonders of its museum. It was once the Palace of the Kings of France. Louis XIV, however, grew weary of the town, and transferred his household goods to Versailles on his way to St Denis, where the royalties of the land now repose in the rigid dignity of death. The rooms are still pointed out where Shemus[17] used to pass his moody hours away, walking with bent frame and tottering footsteps along the oaken floor, and sighing still for the golden bauble of kingship which was never again to come into his possession. Here, too, are chambers sacred to the memory of his unfortunate son the Pretender, who wasted his life away in hunting a shadow and in dreaming Utopian dreams. The chateau itself is of brickwork, and is surrounded by wide and deep ditches arched by picturesque bridges. The apartments are very handsome, and, possessing as they do an historic interest, are always visited by the intelligent traveller.

St Germain, I may add, is now a favourite summer residence of the Parisian. It is, in other words, the Monte Carlo of the dog-days, when its southern prototype, sweltering under the torrid rays of July sun, is deserted for the cooler climes of the North. Nature and Art have combined to embellish the romantic spot. Like Versailles, it has a decidedly Old World air about it. Its edifices, dating back to the Middle Ages, recall the glories of the past to the mind's eye, while its magnificent forest, some five thousand square acres in extent, the marvellous terrace of Leonora, and the Pavilion of Henry IV make it a thing of beauty and a joy for ever. To the Irishman who finds himself in Paris, St Germain ought to be in itself a treasure-trove.

Before the Revolution Paris was for a time the residence of some of our Irish notabilities of that day. The first of these was Richard Brinsley Sheridan, of Dorset-street, Dublin, the wonderful but erratic genius, who rose to be one of the leading orators and dramatists in England. Sheridan's first visit to France was made under rather romantic circumstances. Sheridan had not long left Whyte's learned academy in Grafton Street. He had just only settled down in London when he met and fell in love with Miss Linley, a beautiful young singer of some sixteen summers, in whose honour he used to indite many an amorous poem, full of the fire and enthusiasm of youth. It was of this bewitching cantatrice he wrote the following verse, which has, by-the-by, a refreshing frankness peculiarly its own:

When blest with the smiles of my fair
I know not how much I adore,
Those smiles let another but share
And I wonder I prized them no more.
Then whence can I hope for relief for my woe
When the falser she seems still the fonder I grow.

When the poet and the fair singer met the latter had already been betrothed to an old fogey of some means – a certain Mr Halhead, who, despite the snows of age, worshipped the very ground on which she trod. Seeing, however, that she conceived a passionate attachment to Sheridan, the elderly suitor, with a generosity and self-sacrifice worthy of a Roman, abandoned all claim to the lady's hand and settled the sum of £3,000 on her. Her parents, being of the worldly-wise class, entertained a deep-rooted aversion to giving their daughter to a dare-devil bohemian like Sheridan, but the Irishman decided on making her his wife despite all opposition. With this object he bore her off to Calais, where the interesting couple were married in March 1772. They proceeded from Calais to Paris and resided for some time in the French capital, living rather luxuriously on Mr Halhead's handsome allowance. On their return to England Sheridan forbade his wife to reappear on the stage. The nightingale wished to sing, but the nightingale's owner was inflexible in his determination that she should not sing save in her own house and among her own friends. Mrs Sheridan was a very ambitious woman, and felt the restraint very severely – the result being that the marriage turned out to be a comparative failure. She died, however, in 1792, and some five months afterwards we find Sheridan ingratiating himself into the favours of Madame de Genlis, with the view of obtaining the hand of Pamela, that lady's real or adopted daughter. He was pressing his suit, and with some chances of success, when Lord Edward Fitzgerald crossed his path, and had very little difficulty in dislodging him from Pamela's affections and taking himself the vacant place. Sheridan consoled himself over his loss by marrying, in 1795, Miss Ogle, the daughter of the Dean of Winchester. The second Mrs Sheridan, if report be true, had for years past entertained a tender passion for Lord Edward, and it is said that the hopelessness of her love for the United Irishman was the cause of her early death. May not this state of things in his household be after all the just retribution of fate for the Gallic levity of Sheridan displayed in his lines on 'Love and Marriage':

> Still the question I must parry,
> Still a wayward truant prove,
> Where I love I must not marry,
> Where I marry cannot love.
>
> * * * *
>
> Were she comely ten times over,
> All that heaven to earth allows,
> I should be too much her lover,
> Ever to become her spouse

Verses such as these often come home like curses – to roost. Sheridan, it is unnecessary to add, picked up these eccentric notions in the literary salons of Paris, where he was on several occasions a very prominent and welcome figure.

The Irish Edgeworths were also about this time society lions in the gay French capital. Mr Edgeworth, of Longford, the father of the famous novelist Miss Maria Edgeworth, visited France with his family after the peace of Amiens, and after a tour of Lyons, Marseilles and other provincial cities, settled down for some years in Paris, where his daughter wrote some of her novels and beguiled her leisure hours in a whirl of fashionable life. Miss Edgeworth soon felt the influence of French thought, and became an adept in French epigrammatic conversation, although she never wholly abandoned the more or less rigid conventionalities of her early English training. Among her male acquaintances and admirers were Kosciusko, the Pole, and a Swede named Edelcrantz, an aristocratic and wealthy youth, who began by loving her romances, and wound up by loving herself. He eventually offered his hand in marriage to the Irish girl; but for some reason or another she was induced to decline the offer, although in her subsequent writings, in her *Ennui* and *Leonora*, she gives unmistakable evidence of a romantic attachment to that favoured suitor. It may be remarked, too, that the persistence with which she clung to the 'single state of bliss' in after years was the outcome of her devotion to the same gallant swain. Shortly afterwards a near relative of hers, the well-known Abbé Edgeworth, won a niche in the temple of fame as the chaplain and confessor of the unfortunate Louis XVI, who was the last in the Place de la Concorde to wish that monarch 'God-speed' on his journey to eternity. The Abbé Edgeworth was an Irishman not only by blood, but also by birth. He was born in Edgeworthstown in 1745, and as his father had to emigrate to France, the future priest was educated in the Sorbonne University, where he passed through the usual curriculum with distinguished honours. [. . .] When the monarchy was overthrown, and a Republican form of government was established in its stead, the Irish priest suffered all the penalties of outlawry, but was enabled to secure a safe hiding-place in Choisy, where he remained concealed till sentence of death was passed on Louis XVI, when, with a courage and determination that did him credit, he braved the anger of the law, and rushed to the side of the King on the scaffold in the Place de la Concorde on the ever memorable 21st of January 1793, where he flung his arms around the victim's neck, and is reported to have said, just as the knife of the guillotine pressed the Royal neck, and the Sovereign was being beheaded: 'Louis, son of St Louis, ascend to Heaven!' It has been questioned in certain quarters if the Abbé Edgeworth made use of these words, inasmuch as there is no mention made of them in his autobiography; but it must be remembered that the Irish clergyman was very modest of character and shrunk instinctively from the credit of things which he had nevertheless achieved. It may therefore be looked upon as probable that the phrase alluded to really fell from his lips on the solemn occasion when he was parting from his patron and benefactor. [. . .]

There were in that wretched epoch not a few of our own kith and kin who were treated by the revolutionary party to the tender mercies of the guillotine; but there were others who sympathised with the Mountain Party, and who were as much Red Republicans as any. While the officers of the Irish Brigade, generally speaking, clung faithfully to the Bourbons, a few joined hand in hand with Danton; and other Irishmen, chiefly the new arrivals in France, carried headlong by circumstances and with bitter memories in their hearts of the oppression under which they had groaned at home, became sworn foes of tyranny to the extent of proclaiming that every means were justifiable to establish on a firm basis the power of the people. The divergent opinions of the Irishmen in Paris on this question may be instanced by the fact that after the Abbé Edgeworth, of Longford, had embraced King Louis on that fatal day in the Place de la Concorde, and after the head of that monarch had been severed from the trunk by the pitiless guillotine, Henry Sheares, of Cork, stooped to the ground and sapped his handkerchief in the royal blood, crying out: 'Death to kingly tyranny!' [. . .]

We have now reached the epoch when the leaders of the United Irishmen were beginning to enter into friendly relations with French republicans. One of the first of the former to visit Paris was Lord Edward Fitzgerald. He settled down in an apartment off the Champs Elysées in that city towards the close of October, 1792. Thomas Paine and he soon met in the reunions of the Palais Royal, and as Paine held a high place in the revolutionary councils of the day, Lord Edward soon became initiated into the Jacobin Club and threw himself heart and soul into the republican movement. On November 18th of that year various members of the English and Irish colonies in Paris assembled at White's Hotel to celebrate the victories gained by the armies of France. Mr J. H. Stone occupied the chair on the occasion, and among the toasts drunk with enthusiasm I find the following – 'The Armies of France: may the example of its citizen-soldiers be followed by all enslaved countries till tyrants and tyranny be extinct.' At the same banquet an address was proposed to the National Convention. Citizens Sir Robert Smith and Lord Edward Fitzgerald having addressed the audience and having publicly renounced their titles, the speedy abolition of hereditary and feudal distinctions was proposed and carried by acclaim. For his participation in this republican festival Lord Edward was dismissed from the English army.

Shortly afterwards the United Irishman, going with his friend Stone to a Parisian theatre to see a play called *Lodoiska*, his attention was arrested by the dazzling beauty of a young lady who, in company with two other ladies and a gentleman, sat in a box near his own. After the curtain had fallen he was introduced by Mr Stone to the fair one, who turned out to be Pamela. The birth and parentage of Pamela have been often discussed; but they have not been determined, nor are they ever likely to be. [. . .] In any case, Pamela was brought up in the Orleans household with the other children of the Duke, under the tutelage of their governess, Madame de Genlis. As to the personal charms of Pamela in her early youth, there is no difference of opinion. She is described as one of the most beautiful girls of her time. In the Palace of Versailles the visitor can still see a painting in which she is represented. The canvas is a large one, and the figures are almost life-size. To the right sits Madame de Genlis, twanging her harp, while in the centre is Mademoiselle d'Orleans, also sweeping the strings, and reading from a music-book held by Pamela, whose face is seen in profile. [. . .]

Pamela and Lord Edward were married at Tournay in the beginning of December 1792, in the presence of Madame de Genlis and the Duke of Orléans, afterwards King of France, both of whom signed the marriage deed as witnesses. With the career of the young couple in Ireland we have nothing to do in this paper. It may be only appropriate to mention here that after Lord Edward's death, amongst the papers seized at Leinster House were found some documents proving that his widow had been as deeply implicated as himself in the national conspiracy. The consequence of this discovery was that an order of the Privy Council was issued commanding her to quit Ireland. In 1799 she went to Hamburg with Madame de Genlis. Here she was induced to give her hand to United States Consul Pitcairn, by whom she had one daughter, whose name and place and residence have always remained shrouded in mystery. Pamela's second marriage proved a very unhappy one. Pitcairn was a man of low, grovelling tastes, and constrasted very wretchedly indeed with the gallant Lord Edward. Mrs Pitcairn, finding eventually that it was impossible for her to remain under the conjugal roof, secured a divorce from the American, and having resumed the name of Fitzgerald, she retired to a quiet country retreat in one of the French provinces until the revolution of 1830 raised to the throne the very man who was more than suspected of being her half-brother. Pamela was in consequence of this event tempted to visit Paris, but she received such scanty attentions at the hands of Louis Philippe and his family that she retired to a convent in the suburbs where she died on the 9th of November 1831, at the age of 55, and was buried in the cemetery of Montmartre, the principal mourner at her funeral being Prince Tallyrand. [. . .] Pamela's grave, it must be added, was often visited by Louis Philippe, who appeared to have regretted deeply that he had neglected the desolate lady in the closing years of her existence. Owing to a neglect in the purchase of the grounds of the cemetery, many years subsequently the remains of this once lovely woman were on the eve of being consigned to the 'fosse commune', where the unknown dead of Paris sleep their last sleep, huddled in confusion together, when an Irish resident of Paris discovered the tomb,[18] surrounded by cypress trees; and on a communication being sent to the Duke of Leinster, the remains were transferred to the family vault in the little churchyard of Thames

Ditton, near London, where they now repose side by side with all that is mortal of Lord Henry Fitzgerald, the beloved and faithful brother of Lord Edward. [. . .] It may be added that the marble tombstone on her grave was broken by the bursting of a shell during the siege of 1870. [. . .]

Another United Irishmen of note, Arthur O'Connor, settled down in Paris after the failure of 1798, and, having married the daughter of Condorcet and become a naturalised Frenchman, passed many years of his life under the sunny skies of France, where his children and grandchildren still live, honoured and respected by all who know them. Arthur O'Connor was well and favourably received in French political and social circles, and was regarded as a man of the utmost probity and truth. He believed to the end in the creed of Irish republicanism, although he despaired of the possibility, unless under certain circumstances, of an Irish Republic starting into existence in the course of his own lifetime. O'Connor, who was a general in the French service, passed away at a good old age at his residence, the Chateau de Bignon, on the 25th of April 1852. [. . .]

Bartholomew Teeling, who belonged to an ancient Irish family established in Ulster, was, perhaps, the most ardent of the men of '98. Burning with a desire to take up arms for his country's independence, he embarked for France in order to 'learn the soldier's glorious trade', and entered the army of the Republic under the name of Beron. It is recorded of him that before his final return to Ireland with the French army he paid a secret visit to this country in the interests of the organisation to which he belonged. It was during this visit, it seems, that, according to his nephew, he 'especially won the confidence and affections of Lord Edward Fitzgerald, who became attached to him with all the ardour of his fine nature'. 'I am inclined to think', adds the same authority significantly, 'that there was another of the Geraldines too who took some interest in the fate of the young soldier. I saw a ring which was presented to him by one of them. It is a plain gold hoop, and the characters 'Erin Go Bragh' are inscribed on it . . . He wore it the night previous to his execution, when he sent it to his brother as the dearest pledge he had to leave of fraternal love.' It will be observed that there is in the foregoing paragraph a discreetly veiled hint, which, if put more plainly, must mean that a romantic attachment subsisted between Lord Edward's sister and Bartholomew Teeling. This ring is at present in the possession of Mrs Justice O'Hagan.[19] I must add, however, that one of the living representatives of the family[20] holds the theory that the ring in question was Humbert's gift to his respected ancestor. [. . .]

Robert Emmet resided for some time on two occasions in the French capital. The first occasion was in 1798. He had just then had the honour of being expelled from Trinity College by Lord Chancellor Clare for having in the Historical Society of that institution the courage of expressing his honest republican convictions. The young man had several interviews with the United Irish chiefs then living in the French capital. On the occasion of his second and last visit in the autumn of 1802, Emmet had various consultations with Tallyrand, ex-Bishop of Autun, the then Minister of Napoleon, who seemed very anxious to strike at England through Ireland, despite the fact that both countries were at peace at the time. Napoleon and Emmet also interchanged opinions on the subject; but the former, strange to say, was never very enthusiastic on the project of a French invasion of Ireland. He preferred eventually mooning around the Pyramids, and addressing high-falutin harangues to his troops on the banks of the Nile, to storming Dublin Castle and driving the English red-coats out of Ireland. If he had poured his battalions into this country he would have crushed his arch-enemies, and would never have ended his days crownless and throneless in the ignominious ease of St Helena. While Emmet was endeavouring, but in vain, to persuade the 'Little Corporal' to come to the assistance of the Irish, Thomas Russell and others were preaching the United

Irishman's creed in the pages of the *Argus*, an anti-English newspaper, published in Paris. Week after week Frenchmen were being informed through its columns that Ireland owed no allegiance to the British Crown, and longed for an opportunity to cut the cable that bound her to Britain and establish her independence on a purely republican basis. During this period, Emmet resided with his brother Thomas Addis in the Chateau of Cormeil, near Argenteuil, one of the most pleasant and picturesque of Arcadian retreats around Paris. Up to at least 1885 this chateau was in the possession of the de Castellane family, and was then occupied by the Marchioness of that name, who always spoke of the Emmets as 'les chevaliers Irlandais' – Irish knights of honour, 'sans peur et sans reproche.' A trip to Cormeil ought to interest every Irish tourist, from the fact that around it cluster so many associations of the Emmet family; for even the rooms once occupied by the patriot brothers can still be seen and visited.

Towards the close of the last and the beginning of this century there was one man born of Irish parents in France who rose to the highest position in the land under Napoleon and Louis XVIII. That man's name was Henry Clarke. The son of a humble father and mother, he became Duke of Feltre, and was at one time given over the full control of the Ministry of War. [. . .] Clarke does not seem to have been in particularly good odour with his fellow-Irishmen in France. Wolfe Tone and Emmet speak of him in any but good terms. Indeed his conduct towards several officers of the Irish Legion would warrant one in believing him to be a poor specimen of an Hibernian; for it was by his orders that several sterling Irish soldiers, such as Captains Jackson, Town, Lawless and Miles Byrne, were expelled from French territory for no other reason than that they had remained faithful to the very Napoleonic Eagles of which the Duke himself was supposed to be such a disinterested champion.[21]

The Legion to which these officers belonged had done good service in the cause of France, and was no unworthy successor of the

Irish Brigade, which had been dissolved in 1792. The Irish Legion was established in 1803, as soon as hostilities broke out between England and France, after the brief peace of Amiens. The Irish then in France, seeing in the new situation another possible chance of striking a blow for the deliverance of their country, deputed Thomas Addis Emmet to ask the First Consul to authorise the formation of such a Legion. Napoleon having given the necessary 'imprimatur', Adjutant-General McSheehy was charged to execute the decree and repaired to Morlaix, where he had no difficulty in organising a corps almost exclusively composed of his own fellow-countrymen. Shortly after its formation Captain Tennant and Captain William Corbet were deputed by the Legion to go to Paris to be present at the coronation of the Emperor in Notre Dame. Both officers were presented with a magnificent flag by the newly-crowned sovereign, who thanked the Legion through them for its fidelity to France. On one side of the colours were inscribed the words – 'Napoleon I, Empereur des Francais a la Legion Irlandaise', while on the reverse was a crownless harp, bearing the inscription 'L'independance d'Irlande.' The Irish Legion, it may be furthermore mentioned, was the only foreign corps to which Napoleon entrusted an Eagle.

The career of the Irish Legion in the service of France was worthy of the palmy days of Irish valour and heroism. Throughout France, Germany, Austria, Italy, and Spain they followed the fortunes of the great Commander – not, be it said, so much out of love of the chief, as acting on the hope that he would one day reward their chivalry and self-sacrifice by enabling them to return to Ireland, with his Old Guard, and effect the liberation of that country. That hope, however, proved to be but a dazzling dream. Most of these men, outlaws from the land of their birth, officers who held honourable positions at home before the Rebellion of 1798, peasants and sons of peasants who handled the pike on the slopes of Oulart and on Vinegar Hill, former camp followers of Michael Dwyer on the Wicklow mountains or in the valleys of Imale and Glenmalure – all these and such others were never destined to feast their gaze again on the emerald sward of the isle that bore them. When, owing to Castlereagh's intrigues and English influence exercised through other channels on the Bourbon monarch, the Irish Legion was dissolved in 1815, some of its brave soldiers emigrated to North and South America, and others were drafted into the Foreign Legion. Several of the officers broke their swords in disgust and scattered themselves over the Continent; while others carried their trusty bucklers with them to fresh fields and pastures new in Chili and Peru, where they won fame and wealth and high rank, thanks to their talents and integrity. As the mention of a few of the names of the leading officers of this Irish Legion may be of interest, I give them here: Lieutenant John Sweeny of the city of Cork; Colonel Ware, one of the Kilmainham's former jail-birds; Austin O'Malley of Killala; Captain William Barker, of Vinegar Hill fame; Lieutenant Derry, of the county Down; Lieutenant Pat MacCann of Dublin; Pat Gallagher of the same city, who guarded Lord Edward Fitzgerald from the myrmidons of the 'law' in 1798; Chevalier Terence O'Reilly, and many others well worthy of being included in the glorious beadroll of Ireland's brave soldiers on the continent.

Miles Byrne was perhaps the noblest Roman of them all. Having fought valiantly throughout the entire Wexford campaign of 1798, he was gazetted second lieutenant in the Irish Legion in December, 1803. For 33 years he served under the colours of France, having in 1830 secured the rank of 'Chef de Bataillon'. Byrne lived to a good old age, and was for over a generation the friend and protector of every young Irishman who tried his fortunes in the city of Paris. John Mitchel was a personal friend of his in the French capital in 1860. [. . .]

There is another Irishman, still living and still in exile, old and venerable now, who in the days of his youth and early manhood spent many an hour conversing with Miles Byrne in the Luxembourg

Gardens in Paris. This Irishman, who was a '48 refugee, and who subsequently started a revolutionary movement for Irish independence,[22] was a disciple as well as an intimate friend of the warrior, who received his baptism of fire under Father John Murphy in '98. Thus in the persons of these two exiles was demonstrated the continuity through three links of the Irish national struggle. Miles Byrne died at Paris on the 24th of January 1862, in the eighty-second year of his age, and lies interred in the cemetery of Montmartre, where a befitting slabstone still records the story of his eventful life.

Barry,[23] the Cork painter, resided in Paris for some years before the Revolution. He spent his time in studying masterpieces of art in various galleries of the city, public and private. Personally Barry was a typical illustration of the 'genus irritabile', being ill-humoured, over-sensitive and quarrelsome. His art squabbles in Paris and in Rome show that he was generally always on the warpath, fighting not merely to hold his own corner, but to storm and capture the corners of others. Having lived for some time in Bologna, in Italy, he was elected member of the Clementine Academy of that city, and presented the institution shortly afterwards with a painting, *Philoctetes in the Isle of Lemnos*. After five years spent in Rome, Barry returned to London. Maclise,[24] another Cork painter, was also for several years a familiar figure in the art salons and literary cafes of Paris; while a third Mr Jones[25] was the last representative in the French capital of those artistic abilities that have never failed to bud and blossom on the banks of the Lee. Mr Jones took up his residence in Paris in the beginning of the present decade. He was quite a young man at the time, but gave promise of making his mark one day or another in the profession of his choice. At that time I used to meet the Cork artist occasionally; and it was with very great pleasure indeed that, some years after I had left Paris, I learned that the celebrated portrait painter, Thaddeus, was none other than he. I may add that

Thaddeus's first success was an oil painting, *La Bracconier*, which was deemed worthy of a place in the Paris Salon.

For the first three decades of the present century Paris became the home of a few Irish celebrities, among whom were the Countess of Blessington, Lady Morgan, Thomas Moore and Dr Madden. [. . .] Moore took up his residence in St Cloud, a beautiful suburb of Paris. His cottage lay on a gentle slope overlooking the Seine, quite close to the forest, in the umbrageous depths of which the Irish bard wrote his 'Love of the Angels'. [. . .] Here, too, he commenced his 'Life of Sheridan', and penned some of his delightful Irish melodies. His learned retreat was sometimes broken in upon by visits from Washington Irving, and from many Irishmen in Paris, some of whom must have communicated to him the spirit of a few of his more rebellious poems. On St Patrick's Day, 1820, some of his fellow-countrymen, including Mr Richard Dillon, of Dublin, a '98 refugee, entertained Moore in the restaurant of the Cadran Bleu, on the Boulevards. As, however, the announcement was made that Mr Wellesley Pole Long, nephew to the Duke of Wellington, was to preside on the occasion, Miles Byrne and other Irish officers in the French service declined to attend, for the very good reason that as soldiers who had fought against the English in Ireland, as well as in Spain and Portugal, they would not feel it very agreeable to be listening to speeches and toasts laudatory of the heroes of Waterloo. One of the French officers, however – Lieutenant Tom Warren of Dublin – not having heard of the announcement, was present at the dinner, where everything passed off tolerably well – some of his own inspiriting melodies having been sung by Moore himself – till after the departure of the guest and Mr Wellesley Long, when the parties at table continued the festivities by proposing and responding to the toasts of several well-known Irishmen. When, however, the toast of Reynolds, the infamous informer of '98, who was, strange to say, present on the occasion, was proposed, Lieutenant Warren turned down his glass and asked indignantly if they were to drink to the health of such a dastardly wretch. Confusion immediately reigned around the festive board, the banquet was broken up, and Warren was arrested by a patrol of French police, but was immediately afterwards released on showing his officer's card. The very fact of Reynolds's presence at such a banquet, coupled with the fact more extraordinary still of his toast having been proposed, points to the conclusion that this St Patrick's dinner was rather a feast of flunkeys than an Irish national entertainment. Returning to Moore, it is only necessary to add that he resided in St Cloud from 1819 to 1822, when he returned to England, and spent the remainder of his life in the sweet companionship of his Bessie, to whom, unlike other erratic geniuses caught in the matrimonial web, he proved to be a faithful and devoted husband. [. . .]

Richard Robert Madden, a gentleman to whose historical researches on the '98 movement lovers of Irish literature owe much, spent no inconsiderable portion of his life on the continent. Dr Madden was a native of Dublin and left Ireland in 1820, when he attained the twenty-second year of his age, owing to a pulmonary attack, which necessitated his removal to a sunnier clime. [. . .] Arriving in the capital, he installed himself in a hotel in the Rue Neuve des Bons Enfants, where he felt the smart of straitened circumstances, conceiving at the time a certain delicate aversion to writing to his parents for the sinews of war. After some weeks he succeeded, thanks to his previously acquired knowledge of medicine, in obtaining a situation in an apothecary's shop, on the Boulevard des Italiens, and it was while he held this post that he was introduced to Tom Moore, who was then residing at St Cloud. The French clerks in the 'pharmacie' had no very great love for their young comrade, for he was looked upon, like many another Irishman, as a true-blue son of 'Perfidious Albion'. Things came to a crisis one fine day when one of the French lads, a hot-headed Gascon, and

Madden came to blows. As the average Irishman reaches his best at the fists, Madden proved more than a match for his opponent. The latter, feeling that he must succumb, exclaimed in a white rage, 'Je suis Français', whereupon the other, dealing him a final stroke, cried out, 'Eh bien! Je suis Irlandais', and won the fight.

Madden spent some six months in the apothecary's establishment; but finding the pulmonary disease troublesome once more, he proceeded southwards to Rome by diligence and walked from that city to Naples in a few days. In Naples he joined in practice with Mr Reilly, an eminent Irish surgeon then residing at the feet of Vesuvius. It was here, I believe, he made the acquaintance of Lord and Lady Blessington, to whom during his stay he acted as medical adviser; and it was to a large extent this appointment which enabled him subsequently to write the memoirs of Lady Blessington and her contemporaries – a book which when published took the literary world by storm and evoked the sincere praise of even the most bilious of critics. [. . .]

The late Edmond O'Donovan[26] and John Augustus O'Shea, at present of Paris, could not have held a candle to the worthy doctor as a globe-trotter. He knew the banks of the languid Bosphorus as well as he did those of the fragrant Liffey, and was much at home sitting upon the cedars of Lebanon as he would be while enjoying the cool shade of the elm trees hard by Sandymount. [. . .] The distinguished historian died in Dublin in February 1886, and lies buried in the old churchyard of Donnybrook, sheltered by the very cypress which forty years previously he had had removed from the grave of the Great Napoleon in St Helena and transplanted to the emerald soil of Ireland. As an Irish 'littérateur', Dr Madden has rendered very many valuable services indeed. He has rescued from oblivion many records of the lives of the United Irishmen, and therefore his memory is worthy of all honour in the hands of his fellow-countrymen.

THE IRISH COMMUNITY IN PARIS AFTER 1848

When that patent mediocrity, Louis Philippe, who ruled France with an umbrella instead of with a sceptre, and who abjured the purple of kings for the broadcloth of the 'bourgeois', was hurled from power in the early part of 1848, and a Republic, with the poet Lamartine at its head, was established on the ruins of the Monarchy, the heart of Ireland thrilled once more with hope and confidence. Just as many Irishmen expected aid from France in the preceding generation for the recovery of their national rights, so in '48 there were enthusiasts who fancied that a French expeditionary force, organised for the relief of Ireland, was not merely one of the possibilities but one of the probabilities of the immediate future. An address to the French people, congratulating them on the restoration of a Republican form of Government having been voted at a meeting of the Confederates held in the Music Hall, Lower Abbey-street, Dublin, Smith O'Brien, Thomas Francis Meagher and Hollywood were appointed as delegates to proceed to Paris and offer the congratulations in question to President Lamartine. Hollywood, who was a silk-weaver, was selected in order to symbolise the union of the trades with the Young Irelanders, and to endorse the action of Frenchmen who had raised Albert, the working man, to the post in the new Cabinet as the representative of labour. Although Lamartine, in his *Histoire de la Révolution de 1848*, says that the object of the deputation was to procure arms for an insurrection in Ireland, Sir Charles Gavan Duffy states that it had in view simply the awakening of French sympathy for Ireland. 'They were not', writes the latter authority, 'authorised to negotiate an invasion or even to solicit arms or officers from the provisional government. They would not have placed Ireland under the feet of France any more than under the feet of England . . . But what England did for Flanders, what Holland did for England, what France did for America, France might have done for Ireland – permit and encourage individual citizens to come to her aid. And this is what they expected.'

Richard O'Gorman, Eugene O'Reilly and Lord Wallscourt accompanied the deputation to the French capital, where they were received by Martin McDermott, Paris correspondent of the *Nation*, and by Ledru Rollin, who had some years previously stood on Tara by O'Connell's side, and whose sympathies for Ireland were strengthened by the fact that he had become the husband of an accomplished and patriotic Irish lady. Ledru Rollin was the leader of the French Democrats and played a very important role in the '48 drama. The delegates, escorted by several Irish residents of Paris, presented themselves to the President. The address having been read in French, Lamartine, according to one report, mistook his visitors for English Chartists and thanked them as such for their devotion to the French Republic. According to another authority, the poet of the 'Meditations' made no such mistake, and is reported to have said with peculiar significance: 'Policy imposes a seal on our lips; but our hearts do not throb the less warmly for Ireland.' The British government on this occasion threatened to withdraw the Embassy from Paris if Frenchmen encouraged the Irish agitation, whereupon Lamartine, who belonged to the pap-and-daisy school of maudlin sentimentality, and had none of the stamina of the practical revolutionist in his system, while professing to have infinite good will for Ireland made the humiliating admission that France could not interfere in the internal affairs of the British Empire. This admission was printed by the British Government and posted on all the police stations in Ireland.

After having visited Lamartine, the delegates had somewhat encouraging interviews with Rollin and Louis Blanc, made a round of the popular clubs and paid their respects to the Irish College, where the students, to the number of one hundred, accorded them an enthusiastic ovation. O'Brien, Meagher and O'Gorman addressed the juveniles, who responded with ringing cheers. The president, Dr McSwiney, who was thoroughly adverse to the idea of honouring the Young Ireland chiefs, censured several of the students, seven or eight of whom were under menace of expulsion for nearly a week. One of these latter, it may be added, is now an Archbishop in this country, and is as impenitent an Irishman today as he was in the hot fervour of youth in Paris in 1848.[27] O'Gorman and Eugene O'Reilly remained in the French capital after the departure of the deputation, as Smith O'Brien wished them to acquire in the National Guard as complete a knowledge as possible of military matters. O'Reilly, it may be added, took part in the subsequent insurrection, or rather attempted insurrection, in Ireland, and having escaped to the continent, won his spurs gallantly as Lieutenant of Lancers under Charles Albert of Sardinia, and finally rose to be a commander of a division in the army of the Sultan in Constantinople, where he was known as the O'Reilly Bey.

After the abortive effort in Ballingarry the Irish colony in Paris was recruited by several political refugees, among whom may be mentioned John O'Mahony, James Stephens, O'Donnell, of Limerick; John Walter Bourke, of Cork; and Colonel Michael Doheny. Doheny proceeded from Paris to New York, Burke and O'Donnell returned to Ireland when a Peace of Warsaw reigned in that country, but Stephens and O'Mahony remained for several years denizens of the gay capital. Having established themselves in a pair of snuggeries under the same roof in the very heart of the Latin Quarter, the exiles commenced life under rather adverse circumstances. O'Mahony was in receipt of a small income from a farm near Mitchelstown, which he had given over in trust to his sister, Mrs Mandeville. Stephens was an engineering student on the Great Southern and Western Railway when the call to arms sounded in 1848. O'Mahony became correspondent of an Indian newspaper, to the pages of which he contributed some very interesting letters;

but as no cheques came back in return, he was forced to abandon the pen and seek his fortune in that most precarious of precarious positions, a professorship of English in the French capital. Stephens used also to give lessons; but as he had plenty of time on hands he utilised it by translating several of Charles Dickens's novels into French. All these translations appeared in the feuilleton columns of the 'Moniteur Universel' and were paid for at the handsome rate of three sous a line. Alexander Dumas père and Gustave Flaubert congratulated Stephens on his command over the French tongue, and there is very little reason to doubt the fact that the Irish refugee would have become a distinguished French 'littérateur' if he had pursued a literary career in Paris. His thoughts and dreams were, however, elsewhere. He had stood by Smith O'Brien throughout the ill-fated campaign of 1848; he had been Doheny's companion in a nook amid the crags overlooking Bantry Bay, and sat by Doheny's side while that beautiful song, 'I've Run the Outlaw's Wild Career', was being written; he had dared all for the national cause, and was determined to dare all and do all for it again. Accordingly when he received in 1855 or thereabouts a favourable report from several Irish exiles in America, he determined to fling aside the pen and throw himself into his country's service once more. Stephens resolved to confine his efforts to Ireland, England, and Scotland, while O'Mahony was to work on the American Continent. The name IRB was given to the home organisation; that in America was called the FB, by O'Mahony, who, being an able Irish scholar, bestowed that title on the body in compliment to the memory of Finn and his followers – heroes, we are told, who were taller than Roman spears and whose sinews were cast in iron.

With the subsequent career of Stephens and O'Mahony in Ireland and the United States I have nothing to do. Suffice it to say that Stephens, some months after his escape from Richmond Prison in 1865, returned to Paris, where he had interviews with Emile

Ollivier, Napoleon III's right-hand man,[28] and was received in several salons of the Faubourg St Germain, one of his hosts and intimate friends being the Marquis de Boissy, whose wife, the widow of Count Guiccioli, played such an important part in the life and destiny of Lord Byron. Stephens shortly afterwards proceeded to the United States, but returned to Paris, where, with the exception of another trip westward, he resided until 1885, when, with several other Irishmen,[29] he was expelled from France at the instigation of the British Government, of whom the then French Prime Minister, Jules Ferry, was the abject tool and lacquey. Stephens, who in the meantime had selected Brussels as his residence, had the satisfaction of reading in the newspapers some three weeks afterwards the reports of Ferry's ignoble fall. He resided for some years in the Belgian capital, but has lately returned to Paris on the understanding given by President Carnot that in his case, as well as in those of the Irishmen who were expelled with him, the rights of hospitality on French soil should not be violated a second time. Mr Stephens and his devoted wife now occupy an apartment in the neighbourhood of the Arc du Triomphe, where the war-worn exile leads a life of study and retirement. It is unnecessary to add that he has still as firm a confidence in the ultimate triumph of the national cause as he had in the palmiest days of his eventful career.

The military glory of Ireland's sons did not shine with diminished lustre under the Second Empire. Two of the Marshals created by Napoleon III were the descendants of old Irish families of O'Neill and MacMahon. The former, whose name was Frenchified into Niel, commanded as General the third army corps in 1859, when the French army was sent to help King Victor Emmanuel to drive the Austrians out of Italy. General Niel had commanded and fought with such eminent ability and courage that when peace was concluded he was created a Marshal of France. He had been severely wounded in the campaign, and had suffered besides from the fever of the Italian marshes. One day during his illness a peasant woman brought him a whole basket of wild roses from the Campagna. Niel had always been extremely fond of roses, and as most of them were new to him, they served to amuse him until they were withered. He observed, however, that one particular shoot had not faded and died like the others, but had grown into a beautiful green plant of some ten inches in length. Scarcely knowing why, Niel determined to keep the shoot, and when he returned to Paris he placed it with an expert floriculturist, under whose care it bore next spring four lovely buds of a pale lemon tinge. At that time General Niel was ordered to receive the Grand Cross of the Legion of Honour, symbolic of the highest military rank then known in France, together with his commission of Marshal of France. After the first solemn ceremony was over he went to the reception given by the Empress, who was then in all the perfection of her beauty, and presented to her a curious yellowish rose of artistic shape and dainty perfume, but different from any she had ever seen. After he had told the story of the flower, the dark eyes of Eugenie shone brilliantly as she said – 'Now, Monsieur le Marechal I shall christen this rose for you.' 'Do so', said the Franco-Irish soldier, bowing very low, whereupon the Empress, lightly putting the flower to her lips, exclaimed – 'It is named the Marechal Niel, in hour of the soldier *sans peur et sans reproche*, as gallant in the salon as he is brave on the battlefield!'. Such is the origin of the Marshal Niel rose, which became immediately the fashion in eclectic circles in Paris. Niel cherished the flower to the end of his life, and would not have parted with it for all the gold in the Bank of France. The Marshal had all the characteristic traits of his Franco-Irish parentage, and has left an honourable and imperishable name on the modern military annals of the country which he served so faithfully and so long.

Marshal MacMahon was born on the 13th of July[30] in the quiet chateau of Sully, and was the sixteenth son of Count Maurice

MacMahon, who married a certain Mademoiselle Riquet de Caranam at Brussels in 1792. Young MacMahon having passed with honours through the military academy at St Cyr, was on the 1st of October 1827 nominated to a sous-lieutenancy, and rose from that humble post to the highest position in the State by his own sheer merit and industry alone. His first spurs were won in Algiers, where, at the age of 22, he was awarded the Cross of the Legion of Honour for bravery on the battlefield. On the conclusion of the African Campaign we find Lieutenant MacMahon acting as aide de camp of General Allard at the siege of Antwerp, and winning the epaulettes of Captain. On his return to Africa in 1833 he assisted at the siege of Constantine, and though wounded in the conflict by a splinter from a shell, he nevertheless mounted the breach and was the first to plant the French flag on the ruins of the rampart. At the early age of 34 MacMahon received his brevet of Lieutenant-Colonel in the Foreign Legion, and subsequently exchanged into the 9th Regiment of the Line, when he was ordered to march against the brave Abdel-Kader. MacMahon, in the various engagements in which he took part, was always in the van, and distinguished himself to such an extent that in 1848 he was nominated Brigadier-General. Having been promoted to the rank of General of Division in 1852, he was in August 1854 ordered to proceed to the Crimea; and when Napoleon III, wearied of the protracted length of the siege of Sebastopol, asked Marshal Niel what was the best plan to capture the stubborn town, the Franco-Irishman replied – 'Take the Malakoff, Sire, and Sebastopol is yours!' 'Take the Malakoff' was the order given by the Emperor to another Franco-Irishman, MacMahon, who took the Malakoff and thus hastened the fall of Sebastopol. It is recorded of him that before doing this daring deed he said – 'I will take the Malakoff or I will never leave it alive', and when the bullets were showering around him in the attack, and his aide de camp was begging of him to take shelter from the storm, he observed – 'Do not trouble me; I am surely master of my own skin.' After a long and severe struggle he at last won the day, and announced his victory to the Emperor in the following laconic style: 'J'y suis; j'y reste.' (Here I am, and here I purpose to remain!') When thc campaign was over MacMahon was entrusted with the supreme command of the Army of the Reserve, and was subsequently appointed Senator. When war was declared on Austria by Napoleon III, the Franco-Irish soldier was the man who struck the first fatal blow at the army of Francis Joseph by the splendid and daring capture of Magenta – a triumph which won for him the title of Duke and a Marshal's baton.

His countrymen at home beheld with no small amount of admiration the military success of MacMahon; and when the late Mr A.M. Sullivan started in the *Nation* newspaper a fund with the object of presenting a sword of honour to the newly-created Marshal, the country responded to the call. A sum of £800 was collected. Mr Fitzpatrick, the well-known Irish artist, who is, I believe, at present residing in London, supplied a very handsome design for the sword, the manufacture of which was entrusted to Mr Patrick Donegan, goldsmith and jeweller, of Dame-street. The blade was of the Celtic pattern; it was ornamented with Irish tracery copied from some old Irish manuscripts, and bore the following inscription in French on one side and in Irish on the other: 'Oppressed Ireland to the brave soldier, Patrick Maurice MacMahon, descendant of her ancient Kings.' A deputation left Ireland to present the Marshal with the sword at Chalons. On Sunday, the 9th of September 1860, the presentation took place before the Marhsal's staff and a gallant array of officers, three of whom were Generals of Irish origin. MacMahon replied to the address as follows:

> Gentlemen, I am exceedingly touched by the sentiments which you have addressed to me, and I request you to say to the Irishmen whom you represent how grateful I feel for the testimony of esteem and

sympathy which you offer me in their name. This testimony, by its spontaneous character, has proved to me that the verdant Erin has preserved those chivalrous ideas, that vivacity and warmth of heart which have at all times distinguished her. I shall one day leave to my eldest son Patrick this magnificent sword. It shall be for him, as it is for me, a new pledge of the close ties which ought to unite him for ever to the noble country of his ancestors.

In 1864 MacMahon was appointed Governor-General of Algiers, where he resided till the declaration of war in 1870, when he returned to France. The leading events of that struggle and the important part played by MacMahon at Sedan and subsequently in suppressing the Commune, are so well known, and the record of them so fresh in the memory of the reader, that it would be unnecessary to recapitulate them in this paper. Suffice it to say that MacMahon passed through the campaign with scrupulous honour and integrity. The gallant Irish soldier was elected President of the Republic in 1873, and held that eminent post till the beginning of 1879, when he resigned. Although he was by no means so much at home in the arena of statesmanship as he was under the cover of the tent or on the battlefield, it must be said of him that he was chivalrously loyal to the Republican Constitution, and refused, so long as he was President, to lend a hand directly or indirectly to a Monarchical restoration. Since 1879 he has lived in retirement and seclusion, having exchanged the sword for the pen, and devoting most of his time to his memoirs. If the tocsin of war, however, sounded again, the venerable old Marshal would, I dare say, be found once more in the van.[31]

Under the Second Empire, there were two notable residents of Paris well worthy of mention. One was at one time a prominent Irish politician;[32] the other is at present a member of the Irish Parliamentary Party.[33] The former in the heyday of youth held high revel in the gay capital. He was on one occasion arrested in the Champs Elysées, as he was riding along in a gorgeous equipage drawn by six bays and attended with lacqueys in liveries of green and gold. Having been brought to the police station he was charged with having violated the law by driving in a carriage drawn by six horses, as it was laid down that no person save the Emperor could lay claim to such a privilege. After a few hours' imprisonment, the Irishman was released on the understanding that for the future he should content himself with an equipage of five steeds. The second Irishman alluded to was one of the most remarkable duellists of his day in Paris. The Bois de Bologne, or, in other words, the Belgian frontier, must have witnessed many of his exploits with the pistol or the foil. Although he stood by O'Connell's side fighting the battle of Catholic Emancipation in Ennis in 1828, he is still as hale and hearty and as active and vigorous as any of his colleagues who may happen to be in their fifties.

Among the leading members of the Irish colony in Paris under the Second Empire I might mention the names of Father Prout, John Mitchel, the two O'Donovans – Edmond and William – John Augustus O'Shea and Professor Mortimer Murphy. They all belonged more or less to the Bohemia of literature, and as denizens of that kingdom reflected credit on the land that bore them. Father Prout, whose real name, by-the-by, was Francis Mahony, spent many of his early years on the continent. Trained first in a Jesuit college in France, he proceeded to Rome, where he became an alumnus of the Irish College, and where he penned his immortal poem on the Shandon Bells. Having been duly ordained, he returned to Ireland and commenced his missionary career in the diocese of Cork; but his penchant for profane literature, ill adapted as it was to a conscientious fulfilment of his clerical duties, tempted him shortly afterwards to give up his curacy and try his fortunes in the world of letters in London, where he spent a goodly portion of his life as a contributor to *Frazer's Magazine*, and became an intimate friend of Thomas Carlyle, who, strange to say, had the knack of making many acquaintances among Irish literary men, such as, for example, Gavan Duffy, John Edward Pigot, William Allingham, William J. Fitzpatrick, and others. Prout was for many years in Paris the special correspondent of the London *Globe*. His contributions to that newspaper were the most brilliant literary efforts of the day, and were nearly all written in the reading-room of 'Galignani's Messenger', in the Rue de Rivoli, where John Mitchel used also pen his weekly letters to the Dublin *Irishman* and the New York *Daily News*. Prout was a wonderful linguist, as well as being a wonderful versifier. He translated the 'Groves of Blarney' into Greek and Irish. [. . .] Towards the close of his life, Prout broke his goose-quill and retired to a monastery in one of the suburbs of Paris, where he died in 1868. His remains were afterwards transferred to Cork, and now repose in the Shandon Churchyard within earshot of the bells which owe nearly all their glory to the creative genius of his muse.

John Mitchel resided in Paris on different occasions with his wife and family. His daughter Henrietta, who became a Catholic and joined the Order of the Sacred Heart, died in a convent of that community, and was buried in the cemetery of Montmartre. The Irish colony, however, which had been for years established in Paris, was that in which Professor Mortimer Murphy shone a bright, particular star. Murphy came from the county of Cork. Having reached the Continent early in life, he became in turn a ship carpenter and hotel tout, a champion vaulter in an Austrian circus, and Professor of Hebrew in a college in Hamburg. He acted subsequently as secretary in France to Murphy, the Irish giant, and lectured in Germany on William Shakespeare. While in Brussels he wrote on the staff of the *Indépendance Belge*, and filled the post of tutor to Charles Lever's children on the banks of the Arno. When, after half a lifetime spent in various parts of Europe, he at last settled down in

Paris he became professor of languages, of which he knew thirteen as well as any native. He was for years every evening the centre of a group of Irishmen who used to sip coffee and smoke cigarettes in a nook of the Café Cluny, on the Boulevard St Michel – students of the Sorbonne, political refugees of Young Ireland or the IRB, special correspondents, compositors from 'Galignani', Notre Dame and Pantheon guides, who usually hailed from Munster, and French and German teachers who first saw the light on the pleasant plains of Kildare or in the neighbourhood of the Dublin Coombe.[34] In this select group, the Professor was the observed of all observers. He was a little dapper man, white haired and bespectacled, rather bilious in appearance, but possessing, nevertheless a Corkonian 'bonhomie' of his own which charmed the circle in which he moved. Murphy in those days was an intense republican. Night after night he used to fulminate his thunderbolts on Napoleon the Little and pour withering sarcasm on the Napoleonic regime. His choler was, however, at no time raised to such a pitch as it used to be when one of the Irish boys would whisper that the Emperor meditated conferring on him the ribbon of the Legion of Honour, for Mortimer had as much contempt for honours as Colonel John Hay, who wrote: 'As the meek beasts in the Garden came flocking for Adam to name them, men for a title today crawl to the feet of a king!'

So vast was the Professor's store of general information that he was known in the Latin Quarter as a walking encyclopædia. John Augustus O'Shea was another luminary in the same orbit. The Irish Bohemian was John Mitchel's successor as Paris correspondent of the *Irishman*, and lived for a long time in the Pension Bonnery, Rue de Lacépède, near the Jardin des Plantes – a French boarding-house, most of the boarders of which were Irishmen, among them being Nick Walsh, the painter, who was arrested in Dublin in 1865 on suspicion of being James Stephens; William O'Donovan, alias William Hamilton, correspondent of the *Irish Times*;[35] Alfred O'Hea, a medical student, who subsequently became a newspaper editor in Castlebar, where he died of consumption; and Edmond O'Donovan, of Merv and Soudan fame.[36] Of these, O'Shea and William O'Donovan subsequently shared the privations of the Paris siege in common. [. . .]

Among the other Irishmen who resided for a time in Paris may be mentioned Sir Charles Gavan Duffy, whose fixed residence of late years has been Nice; the late Denis Florence McCarthy, who used to patronise the Continent from Boulogne-sur-Mer to Naples; General Phil Sheridan,[37] who was the guest of the German Emperor and Prince Bismarck throughout the Franco-German War; Mackay, the famous Limerick millionaire, who offered to illuminate the Arc du Triomphe one night at the cost of several thousand pounds in honour of his step-daughter's marriage with Prince Colonna, but whose offer was respectfully declined by the municipality; and John Savage,[38] the poet of the Dodder, who loved the welcome shades of the Luxembourg Gardens, and who wrote several of his poems while rusticating in the forests of St Cloud.

Here I may be permitted to have a few words to say in regard to the Irish company which took part in the Franco-German campaign.[39] Thanks to the exertions of Mr A. M. Sullivan and others, one hundred men, chiefly Dubliners, proceeded to France after the fall of Sedan under the guise of an ambulance corps, and took service in the French army. Captain Kirwan was the commanding officer of the company, his two lieutenants being Cotter and McAlevy. Martin Hanley Carey became later on a lieutenant in the same body. The Compaigne Irlandaise, as it was called, fought on the banks of the Loire, and was subsequently driven, with Bourbaki's army, into Switzerland. The bravery of its members throughout the campaign won them the encomia of all their superior officers.

In a list of the prominent members of the present Irish colony in Paris the name of Mr Michael Morphy must not be omitted. Morphy was born of Irish parents in the very heart of Montmartre, some twenty-four or twenty-five years ago. His early surroundings fostered in him that wild spirit of anarchy which eventually grew so strong that even while still a boy he mounted platform after platform in Belleville, and denounced in all the moods and tenses the 'capitalists who were living on the vitals of the people'. Morphy was in those days a full-blown rebel against society. He used to arouse the enthusiasm, or, might I rather say, the rapacious greed, of many by picturing for their mental gaze the glad and glorious time coming when the wealth of a nation will not be monopolised by the few, but shared equally by all. If Morphy had confined himself to these idle speculations he might still have remained in his original obscurity; but he went a little farther and began to talk ominously of traitors' heads, hempen cords, and lamp-posts with all the boyish ardour of a Marat in bib and tucker. Extravaganzas such as these in his speeches attracted the attention of the government 'mouchards', who soon discovered that this hot-headed foolish boy was a foreigner and as a foreigner could be summarily expelled according to law from French territory if his presence were considered dangerous to the common weal. Morphy was accordingly shown the door and was landed politely on the other side of the frontier. The next returning train, however, brought him back to Paris, where he was immediately arrested for having driven a coach-and-four through the Ministerial decree in his regard. He was brought before the Tribunal and sentenced to three months' imprisonment in St Pelagie, on the expiration of which term he was once more expelled the country. The irrepressible youth returned in hot haste by the next train, was again arrested, and again imprisoned. This bit of stage play was renewed no less than four times, until Morphy attained his majority, when, taking advantage of the statute that enables children born of foreign parents on French soil to opt for French nationality when they reach the twentieth year of their age, he proudly proclaimed himself a citizen of France, and could no longer be molested. Morphy's popularity grew, of course, with the persecution of which he was the victim. Lately, however, a change has come over the spirit of his dreams. He seems to have sown the last of his wild oats, politically speaking, for his is now one of Boulanger's right hand men in Paris; and if the brave General comes to power next November,[40] we may expect to find this adventurous Irishman a prominent member of his cabinet.

Another adventurous Irishman, the Baron Harden Hickey, is also a well-known member of the Irish colony. The Baron is as rabid a royalist as Morphy is a rabid republican. Hickey became editor and proprietor of a French comic print called *Le Triboulet*, in which he lashed the government with such 'verve' and vigour that he, too, was expelled from the precincts of the Republic. Some years ago, however, he returned to Paris and having taken out his papers as a French citizen he can now defy the authorities. Of the descendants of the old Irish, Viscount O'Neill de Tyrone is the most prominent figure. He has translated many of Moore's melodies into French, and takes part annually in the St Patrick's Dinner of the anciens Irlandais – the banquet of the modern Irish being attended exclusively by Hibernians born on the green soil.[41] Among the others may be mentioned Count O'Connell, Count O'Mahony, and 'tutti quanti', all of whom cherish a true and faithful love for the island of their birth or ancestry.

We may wind up our Irish footprints in Paris with brief notices of Schiller's printing office, the Church of the Passionist Fathers, and the Irish College. Schiller's printing office, situated in the Rue Montmartre, within a stone's throw of the bustling boulevards, was for some two months the haunt of many Irishmen in Paris owing to the fact that it was here where *United Ireland* was edited and printed after it became proscribed in Dublin under the Forster regime. It was the first occasion on which an Irish newspaper was produced in Paris,[42] and its appearance in that city caused such a flutter in the Downing-street dovecot that the emissaries of Scotland Yard were sent over in battalions to keep watch and ward over the dangerous office, and look after everybody connected with it, from Mr Patrick Egan, the director, down to the merest printer's devil on the premises.[43]

The Church of the Passionist Fathers, in the Avenue Hoche, is the Sunday rendezvous of many members of the Irish colony. Standing outside that edifice after High Mass, on any given Sabbath, one finds himself listening to the old familiar accents of the four provinces – to the hard clink of the North, and the mellifluous brogue of the South; while Leinster and Connaught are also proportionally represented in the chorus.

In a small narrow street, the Rue des Irlandais, quite close to the Pantheon, stands the Irish College. Over the door of the establishment one sees the outlines of a harp surrounded with oak branches and palm leaves, and surmounted with the inscription, 'College des Irlandais'. On a black marble slab in the hall is a list of the benefactors of the College, among whom are the names of Louis XIV, Right Rev. Dr O'Mahony, Bishop of Limerick; the Baron de Lescalpier, and the Rev. Malachi Kelly. The hall is painted in panels of marble, and above, on a green ground in gold letters, are the words 'France-Ireland: Armagh, Dublin, Tuam and Cashel'. In the antechamber is a list of the Irish prelates who read their courses, or read part of their courses, in the establishment, among them being the name of the illustrious Archbishop of Cashel. The rector, Dr MacNamara, is a genial elderly gentleman, and one of the professors is Dr MacHale, the nephew of the 'Lion of the Fold of Judah'.[44] There are about one hundred students in the College at present. The professors are nominated by the Minister of Education on the recommendation of the Archbishop of Paris; while the income of the institution is derived from the property it owns in Bordeaux and from the old Lombard College.

The Irish College of Paris dates from the last quarter of the sixteenth century. Father Lee and a band of Irish exiles settled in the French capital some three hundred and ten years ago. Having no financial resources of their own, they were installed in the College of Montaigue. This was the home of Irish students for many years. The diet in the establishment was scant and poor. Meat and wine were conspicuous by their absence from the 'festive' board, beans, haricots, and herrings forming the dishes of each repast, half a herring being the allowance of each of the younger boys, while a whole one fell to the lot of each of the elders. Fish, it is said, supplies the brain with phosphorus; and it may have been this ichthyophagous fare that contributed to a certain extent to the success achieved by the Montaigue juveniles at the University of Paris. The Irish students migrated in 1605 to the aristocratic College of Navarre, while a branch house was taken in the Rue de Sevres, from which they were eventually transferred to the College des Lombards, which was handed over to them exclusively by Louis XIV. The College des Lombards had, it may be observed, been previously inhabited by Ignatius of Loyola and St Francis Xavier. It continued for over a hundred years to afford shelter and a home to many a brave Irishman.

The Paris Irish College of our day is only one hundred and twenty years old. It was built by the then Prefect of Studies, the Rev. Laurence Kelly, in the Rue de Cheval Vert, now Rue des Irlandaise, in 1770. In 1792, during the Reign of Terror, it fell under the same ban as other ecclesiastical institutions, and its Superior, the Abbé Kearney, who, with the Abbé Edgeworth, had been present at the execution of Louis XVI, was thrown into prison, and narrowly escaped being guillotined. When the troubled days of the Revolution passed away the doors of the College were again thrown open, and Napoleon I expressed a wish that the sons of the old Irish families settled in France be sent there. Many of the Dillons and the O'Sullivans, the Blakes and the O'Donnells responded to the call, and were followed by scions of the French noblesse. It may be interesting to recall to mind the fact that on its rolls can be seen the names of Jerome Bonaparte, afterwards King of Westphalia, and father of the present Prince of that family; Baron Shee, Commander Corbett, and four Counts de la Rochefoucauld. The Irishmen's sons who were provided with bourses received an excellent education at the time, for they had the advantage of following the classes at the Lycée Napoleon, then in high repute for its able professors. Among its most distinguished students were Messrs MacMahon, O'Brien, MacSheehy, O'Moran and O'Mara. Then came the disasters of 1814, when the College, after the restoration of the Bourbons, had to undergo many changes. The Irish Catholic bishops having endeavoured to get all the property belonging to the Irish seminaries in France transferred to Ireland, to be annexed to Maynooth College, a protest against such a project was signed by nearly all the Irish officers in the French service on the plea that the step in question would be a violation of the testators' intentions. The French Government refused to accede to the request of the Irish Episcopacy, and the Irish College was consequently spared. It was shortly afterwards conducted by an official commission composed of Marshal MacDonald, Grand Chancellor of the Legion of Honour; Lally Tollendal, a peer of France; Lieutenant-General Count O'Mahony, and Dr MacMahon.

Some interesting anecdotes are told of the Abbé Kearney, who at one time presided over the establishment. One of these is recounted by Miles Byrne: 'The Abbé Kearney was always gay and good-humoured, never speaking harshly of anyone. He was low in stature, well made, with a very agreeable and benevolent countenance. He had very little to live on before he became superior of the Irish College, and still with that little he was ever endeavouring to be useful to his friends and countrymen. I met him one day with a rather large parcel under his arm; he told me it was one of his pantaloons he was taking to a poor exile of Erin. He hoped it would fit him, for he (the Abbé) was to present him at ten o'clock to a French family, where he expected to have him installed as tutor or preceptor.' Succeeding presidents such as Dean Ryan, of Cashel; Father Magrath, of Waterford; Dr MacSweeny, of Carlow, and others conducted the affairs of the College with the utmost tact and ability. During the Revolution of 1848 barricades were thrown up in the Rue des Irlandais, but the Revolutionists were dissuaded by one of the professors, the Abbé O'Loughlin, from entering the precincts, on the plea that it was a purely Irish institution. During the Second Empire all the Irish foundations in France were placed under one jurisdiction, the special supervision of the Irish College being given to the Archbishop of Paris and the Irish bishops. Since 1873 the organisation is regulated by a decree of M. Jules Simon, the then Minister of Public Instruction. Its administrative board is composed of seven members, three of whom are judges of the superior courts of the State, three nominated by the Minister, the seventh being the Superior of the College. The functions of the board, it may be added, consist in controlling the budget, the expenses and the revenues. [. . .]

The places of interest for Irishmen in the remainder of France are somewhat few, among which may be numbered the town of Rennes, where several valuable Gaelic MSS are preserved; Tours, the alleged birthplace of St Patrick; and Savoy, in the fastnesses of which Lord Mountcashel's[45] brigade achieved a glorious triumph for the Bourbon flag over the Piedmontese.

Chapter 3

Italy, Iberia and Central Europe

IRISH FOOTPRINTS IN SWITZERLAND AND ITALY

The Irish associations of Switzerland must not be omitted in a series such as this purports to be. In the war just alluded to between the French and Piedmontese, the Irish, comprising as they did nine battalions, fought chiefly against the soldiers of the Pays de Vaud. Catinat, the French Commander-in-Chief, being sorely harassed by these Swiss Mountaineers, who hated the French – thanks to the revocation of the Edict of Nantes[1] – ordered the Irish to attack them in their fastnesses. The Irish, accustomed as they had been to chase the wild deer over the Comeragh mountains and the peaks of Slievenamon at home, pursued the Vaudois through the lonely defiles of the Alpine hills, displaying in these perilous excursions their wonted bravery and powers of endurance. The triumph of the Irish was complete. They not only saved the French army from destruction, but carried terror and dismay into the camp of the enemy. The memory of this incursion into Switzerland has rendered the Irish name and nation odious to the Vaudois.

A more agreeable Irish souvenir connected with the Pays de Vaud is, however – despite the fact just recorded – the hospitality accorded in the canton years afterwards to a few score officers of the Irish

Brigade who were expelled from France in 1792 by the Revolutionary Committee for their devotion to the Bourbons. These exiles pitched their tents on the banks of Lake Leman. Some resided in Lausanne, others occupied chalets over-topping the vine-clad hills that extend from the town to Montreux, quite close to the old prison of Chillon, in a locality endeared to the scholar by so many literary and romantic associations. In this delightful retreat, where the azure blue of the lake vies with the cerulean tints of the skies overhead, they spent twenty years of their chequered lives. From their place of refuge they could see across the sheet of water the hills of Savoy towering to the clouds and guarding the land from which they had been ruthlessly banished. In this 'exile's exile' of theirs they were not, however, quite alone. They were welcomed in several social circles. Lord Cloncurry,[2] who was then at school at Lausanne, gives us a graphic picture of those refugees, whom he describes as not only soldierly but handsome in appearance. Not a few of them were the sons of Irish fathers and French mothers – a circumstance which warrants his lordship as well as other authorities to come to the conclusion that the intermingling of French and Irish blood is in almost all cases certain to produce very fine specimens of the human race; for these latter possess as a rule the characteristics and qualities of the peoples of both nations, the vigorous physique, the wit and gaiety of the Irish, combined with the finesse, the grace, and affability of the average Frenchman.

Apropos of Lausanne, it may be added that O'Connell visited the town in 1847, and stayed at the old Hotel Gibbon, an establishment which, it may be interesting to note, was built on the very site of the house where the celebrated English historian wrote many pages of the *Decline and Fall of the Roman Empire*.[3] When the news of O'Connell's arrival became known, large crowds of enthusiastic Swiss crowded in front of the hotel, from the balcony of which they were addressed by the Irish Tribune in academical French; for

O'Connell had by no means forgotten a language the rudiments of which he had mastered some fifty-five years previously in the colleges of Douai and St Omer. His reception at the hands of the Lausannois took on the same evening the shape of a serenade – a torchlight procession having been formed to do him honour.

St Gall is another Irish landmark in Switzerland, and is called after an Irish saint of that name. St Gall was born in Ireland in 551, and having been educated in Bangor, followed St Columbanus to France. He eventually proceeded to Switzerland, where, on the banks of Lake Constance, he founded the famous monastery of Arbon. Here he worked might and main to combat and crush Paganism, with the result that he converted thousands to Christianity, and won for himself the title of one of the chief Apostles of Switzerland. After a long and laborious life he died in this locality in 640. Relics of the saint are still enshrined in the cathedral of St Gall, which is now one of the most flourishing towns in the Federal Republic.

Crossing the Alps we find ourselves in the pleasant plains of Lombardy. Here several well-fought fields speak to the Irishman of Marshal Niel and Marshal MacMahon. The Foro Bonaparte in Milan, where the French army, headed by MacMahon, was received by the Emperor on the occasion of the final triumph over the Austrians, well deserves a visit; while the plain of Magenta, the scene of one of the Marshal's greatest victories, is situated in the immediate neighbourhood. Genoa is associated with Irish annals as the city where O'Connell breathed his last. Tourists can still visit in that city the hotel where he died in 1847. This establishment is called the Hotel Feder, one of the outer walls of which contains a circular niche where a bust of O'Connell still stands, underneath being an inscription in Latin, which may be translated into English as follows: 'To Daniel O'Connell, the Champion of Civil and Religious Liberty of his own Ireland, who, while on his way to Rome, departed this life in this house on the Ides of May, 1847. This memorial, erected by subscription, in the hundredth year of his birth, 1875.' Some years ago the Very Rev. Canon Brosnan, PP of Cahirciveen, County Kerry, who is at present engaged in erecting an O'Connell Memorial Church in that locality, visited the hotel on his return from Rome, where he had an interview with his Holiness Leo XIII. [. . .]

Rome perhaps of all the cities of the Continent can boast of the largest number of Irish associations. Sitting on a gently sloping eminence quite close to the Piazza di Spagna, and removed from the din and clamour of the Corso, is the Irish Franciscan Monastery of San Isidore. The church is surmounted in front on either side by two statuettes, one to the right representing San Isidore, and that to the left St Patrick. The Apostle of Ireland wears the episcopal mitre, and holds a crozier in his right hand. For two hundred and sixty years this monastery has been in the hands of the Franciscan Fathers of the Irish Province. It is endeared to the Irish heart by a thousand and one touching souvenirs; for as long as it stands on the Pincian Hill it will recall to the memory of the wayfarer from the Emerald Isle 'those Penal days, those Penal days, when godless persecution reigned', and when many an Irish refugee found shelter and hospitality within its precincts. [. . .] During my residence in Rome I paid several visits to this historic Irish house. The coats of arms of Munster, Leinster, Ulster, and Connaught looked from the interior of the old walls. Guided by an Irish cicerone, I proceeded on one occasion into a little garden hard by, from whence we plunged into the subterranean vaults of San Isidore, where the air was as chilly as that of Siberia, and as musty as that of an antiquary's library. Here in the flickering light of a solitary taper we saw many an Irish mausoleum, stone coffins containing the remains of Irish priests and soldiers; epitaphs that spoke to us of the devotion and chivalry of the Gael; tablets that reminded us we were surrounded by the ashes of Hibernians who came hither from every nook and corner of the old land. Here, too, lie buried many of the Franciscan fathers themselves. Now, however, no sepulture is possible within the precincts of San Isidore, for under the new regime all the dead must be buried outside the walls. The church attached to the establishment is full of Irish souvenirs. In front of the high altar a marble slab let into the floor covers the last resting-place of Luke Wadding, while in the abundance of rich marble, gilded stucco, and paintings that greet the eye on all sides are several mural tablets erected to the memory of Irishmen and women. One of these commemorates Amelia Curran (the sister of Sarah), who died in the extreme south of Italy. The inscription runs as follows: 'AMELIA CURRAN, the most talented and virtuous daughter of JOHN PHILPOT CURRAN, who fearlessly espoused the cause of his country and his oppressed fellow citizens before corrupt judges and hostile juries. THEY WERE TRUE PATRIOTS. To their memory this tablet is inscribed by their surviving friend, VALENTINE SECOND LORD CLONCURRY, Anno Domini, 1848.'

There is another monument in the church invested with the glamour of romance. It is reared to the memory of Miss Octavia Bryan, at one time a leading belle in the fashionable salons of Rome. This Irish lady was, it seems, engaged to be married, and on the eve of her wedding day she happened to attend a ball given by a Roman prince, where she danced all night long with the usual light-hearted and bouyant disposition of a daughter of the Emerald Isle. On returning home she was seized with fever, and died a few hours subsequently, just at the moment when the nuptial ceremony was to have taken place. Her friends crowned the lovely head with a wreath of orange flowers, veiled the delicately pale face, and draped her figure in the robe of snowy white which she was to have worn as a bride. Thus attired, she was laid in a coffin and consigned to the grave. She had barely attained the twentieth year of her age, and was mourned by all who knew her. A recumbent statue of the maiden, crowned with roses, surmounts the monument reared to her memory.

The Theological Hall of San Isidore is well worth a visit. Its walls are painted in fresco – the work of a lay brother, Emmanuel of Como, who toiled for the weal and glory of his order here some two hundred years ago. Among the portraits in the frescoes are those of Thomas Fleming, Florence Conry, Hugh MacCaghwell, Maurice de Portu of Tuam, Anthony Hickey, John Colgan of Louvain, and John Ponce. The two finest specimens of the lay brother's art are undoubtedly the realistic portraits of Duns Scotus and Luke Wadding. The fresco, however, that possesses the most interest for Irishmen is that in which Luke Wadding, Ponce, Hickey, and Harold are represented working together in the library of San Isidore on *The Annals of the Franciscans*. [. . .]

The founder of San Isidore was certainly one of the most brilliant scholars of his age. He was born in Waterford in 1588, his father, Walter Wadding, being a merchant in that city, and his mother, Anastasia Lombard, being a near relative of the illustrious Peter Lombard, Archbishop of Armagh. He left Ireland early in life, and at the age of fifteen became an alumnus of the Irish Seminary of Lisbon, where he studied philosophy under the Jesuits. He shortly afterwards entered the Franciscan Convent at Matozinhos, near Oporto, in Portugal, and having been duly ordained, proceeded to Coimbra, where Dr Doyle, the celebrated J. K. L., studied at one time. Here Father Wadding preached eloquent sermons in Portuguese, and otherwise distinguished himself as an excellent Greek, Spanish, and Hebrew scholar. He reached Rome at the age of thirty years as companion to the Bishop of Carthagena, who was investigating the theology of the Immaculate Conception, and who required the services in this inquiry of such an eminent divine as Wadding was held to be even then. Wadding on this occasion resided in the Franciscan Convent of St Peter in Montorio, in the church attached to which, some short time previously, the bones of O'Neill and O'Donnell, the banished earls, were laid to rest. For his great literary labours he consulted the Vatican archives and other libraries in Rome, and journeyed to Perugia, Assisi, and Naples in search of materials. His chief work is entitled *The Annals of the Franciscan Order*, and was undertaken by him in obedience to his superiors. He was engaged over this volume for twenty years, and managed to secure for its compilation piles of manuscripts from all nations in Christendom. [. . .] Nor was he in the midst of his studies forgetful of the land of his birth or of her claims on his loyalty and devotion. He solicited, we are told, and procured supplies of money, arms and expert Irish officers from France and Flanders to be sent to Ireland before the so-called rebels had any thoughts of demanding them. For this assistance he received the warm thanks of the Supreme Council then established in Kilkenny. In 1642 he was commissioned to act as Irish agent to the Pope, Cardinals, and other princes of Italy, and was chiefly instrumental in supplying the Irish at home with arms and ammunition for the struggle in which they were engaged. Despite the fact that he was one of the greatest men of his day, he was in character and demeanour very modest and retiring. As a proof of this, it may be mentioned that when a deputation went from this country to Rome to request Pope Urban VIII to make Luke Wadding a cardinal, the learned Franciscan got possession of the document containing the request and took very good care that it never was presented to the Pontiff. Among the more remarkable Irish Franciscans who were either contemporaries or successors of Luke Wadding in San Isidore was Patrick Fleming, of Louth, first professor of Philosophy and afterwards a guardian and lecturer in Divinity at Prague, where he died a martyr to the Faith. Hugh MacCaghwell was remarkable for the cult with which he honoured the memory of Duns Scotus, whose nationality he demonstrated to have been Irish. He was, it may be added, part founder with Florence Conry, Archbishop of Tuam, of the Franciscan College of St Anthony at Louvain. Among the other eminent Irishmen of the Order were Paul

King, a philosophical writer; James Miles, a native of Drogheda; Bonaventure Baron, alias Fitzgerald, a native of Clonmel who was considered the first Latinist in Rome and the most enthusiastic champion of the theology of Scotus; Francis Porter from Meath; and Francis Bermingham from Galway, who filled the chair of Philosophy with distinction in Milan – all of whom were at one time or another connected with the College of San Isidore.

The North American College in the Via dell'Umilità may be looked on as another of the Irish establishment in Rome, for nearly all its students are Irish either by birth or parentage. When in 1859 Irish-American scholars came to the city of the Seven Hills and sought an asylum for religious study, they selected as their home the old deserted palace of the Orsinis, situated in the street just referred to, quite close to the lower and western base of the Quirinal. How many centuries the Orsini generations followed each other in this venerable pile history cannot tell; but it has for the last thirty years come to pass that where once rang the gay revelry of the patrician dance and song now walks the cloistered student. An Italian porter guards the massive door of the College. Entering the open court the visitor makes his way to the reception room, the walls of which are adorned with portraits of eminent ecclesiastics, in the midst of which can be seen a fine large steel engraving of Washington, as well as equally large engravings of the Holy Cross of Boston and St Patrick's Cathedral in New York. There was also a large well-framed statement concerning the founder of the College, from which it appears that the institution owes its existence to the munificence of Pope Pius IX, and was formally opened on the 7th of December, 1859, for the reception of students. Without the reception-room is a green courtyard, in the centre of which stands a palm tree keeping watch and ward over a sparkling fountain. Mounting the spiral staircase one sees exquisite copies of master paintings on the walls. On the whole, the College is a tasteful and well-appointed establishment.

Its object is to furnish American Catholic students of special promise with facilities for advanced study at the very ecclesiastical centre of the Faith, and to prepare them for missionary work in their own country.

There are at present upwards of seventy students residing in the seminary. Little instruction is given in the College itself, its main work being in the line of discipline and direction; for the lectures must be attended by the alumni at the Propaganda, where the various departments of Languages, Theology, Ethics, Church History, and Canon Law are presided over by distinguished ecclesiastics. The American College has supplied the United States with most of its bishops and eminent priests. Dr Glynn, of New York, must be ranked among its children, few in number, who rebelled against the Vatican.[4] Its country house is situated on the delightful Alban Hills, where the students play base-ball and indulge in all kinds of American sports in vogue. The present rector, Monsignor O'Connell, though young in years, has already attained a prominent position in the Eternal City, and is distinguished alike for his learning and zeal. It is satisfactory to be able to add that the Irish students of the North American College hold more than their own in the learned halls of the Propaganda, and manage every year to bear off quite a respectable number of doctors' caps.

The Irish College in Rome is situated on the declivity of the Quirinal Hill, and is tenanted by some sixty students who hail from different portions of Ireland. Its president is the well-known Dr Kirby, Archbishop of Ephesus *in partibus*[5] – a venerable ecclesiastic, who has passed over half a century of his life on the Continent, the greater portion of that period having been spent in the Eternal City. Monsignor Kirby is a slightly-built, ascetic-looking gentleman, modest and unassuming in manner, yet possessing that dignity and courtly reserve which characterised the Irish priests educated in Continental schools. His Grace converses in English slowly and with a certain hesitation, from which it would not be difficult to conclude that he is on more familiar terms with the Tuscan than with the Anglo-Saxon tongue. The infirmities attendant on extreme old age have of late prevented Monsignor Kirby from devoting himself as he would wish to his duties as rector of the institution, but at the time I had the honour of having an interview with him – now some three years ago – he was ably and effectively assisted by his coadjutor, Dr Verdon, the late president of Clonliffe. His Grace, I need hardly add, takes a keen and profound interest in the welfare of his native land, and never misses an opportunity of championing her cause within the precincts of the Vatican, where, as Papal Chamberlain, he wields a widespread and well-merited influence.

The Church of St Agatha, attached to the College, will have a peculiar interest for Irishmen visiting Rome, owing to the fact that here lies enshrined the heart of Daniel O'Connell. This relic of the Tribune reposes near the high altar against the wall of the left isle and is encased in monumental marble, one of the bas-reliefs of which represents the Irishman as he stood at the bar of the English House of Commons in 1829, in the act of refusing to take the oath. [. . .] It may be added that the Church of St Agatha and the buildings adjoining it were assigned by Pope Gregory XVI as a residence for Irish students during the rectorship of the late Cardinal Cullen. Previous to that epoch the Irish students resided in a venerable edifice in another portion of the city, where one day, during the siesta, young Francis O'Mahony, afterwards Father Prout, penned his immortal lines on the Bells of Shandon. [. . .]

The Irish Domincian Church of St Clement is situated in the street leading from the Coliseum to the Lateran, and is one of the earliest Christian basilicas of Rome. The interest attached to it is enhanced by the fact that in 1857 Father Mulhooly, the worthy Prior, accidently discovered a subterranean church situated at a level of twenty feet below the modern building. We are told by Father MacCartan that so interesting was this discovery considered in Rome that Pius IX encouraged Father Mulhooly to proceed with the excavations and gave large contributions for that purpose. The aisles and nave have been cleared out, and the church now stands forth as it was when erected, probably about the end of the fourth century. It may be interesting to note that it was to the oratory of St Clement the mangled remains of Ignatius Bishop of Antioch, one of the first martyrs of the Flavian amphitheatre, were conveyed. Here, too, was the doctrine of Pelagius condemned by Pope Innocent about the year 415, and Pelagius himself excommunicated.[6] This subterranean church is brilliant illuminated on the Feast of St Clement. In the present modern church, which was erected in the beginning of twelfth century, stands a choir enclosed by marble walls, on which are sculptured in exquisite style various Scripture emblems and the monogram of Pope John VIII. Altogether the Irish Dominican Convent of Rome is one of the most interesting structures in the Eternal City.

The Irish Augustinians have also a house in Rome, or rather are building one – their former convent having been appropriated by the Italian Government. Attached to the new building will be erected a church in honour of St Patrick, a project which has been already set on foot by the able and energetic Prior Glynn. One of the most distinguished of the Irish Augustinians in Rome is Father Locke, brother of the late John Locke, the Irish poet,[7] who has written so many charming national ballads. Father Locke has attained to the high position of the Professorship of Hebrew in the Propaganda, and is ranked among the most accomplished linguists on the banks of the Tiber.

Among the learding members of the Irish lay colony of Rome I may mention Mr P.L. Connellan and the Commendatore Cassell. Mr Connellan is a veteran Irish-Italian. Though born and reared in Ireland, he has the bronzed features of a native of the sunny South. The hot suns of some twenty-five Italian summers may have changed his complexion and made it, so to speak, racy of the soil, but they have not changed his Irish heart. The Italian language ripples from his tongue with all the accuracy and volubility of a genuine Florentine contadino, but the tongue has not on that account lost the flavour of the mellow Irish brogue. Mr Connellan has his entrées into the Vatican, and is one of the most reliable and the best informed of foreign correspondents in Rome. He is the representative of a Boston Irish and Catholic newspaper,[8] and was, I am happy to add, one of those staunch Irishmen who trod on Sir George Errington's toes when that toady was creeping up the back stairs of Pope Leo's residence, and was endeavouring to 'humour' the Vatican by defaming the character of the Irish people. Commendatore Cassell is also held in high repute in the Vatican, where he holds an official position in the Pope's entourage. The Commendatore is also a pressman, being the special correspondent of one of your Dublin contemporaries. These and other members of the Irish colony, lay and ecclesiastical, have their annual banquets and reunions on St Patrick's Day. Sermons appropriate to the occasion, and dealing, of course, with the old land and her national hopes and aspirations, are preached on that day in San Isidore, St Clements, and St Agatha, while the evening is celebrated by a banquet in the refectory of the Irish College, presided over by the venerable Archbishop Kirby, among whose guests one may find a Cardinal, a few Monsignors from the Vatican, and other distinguished ecclesiastics, all of whom drown the trefoil in friendly rivalry with the Irish who may happen to be present at the festivity.

There is, however, in Rome, as there is on the banks of Lake Leman, another Irish colony of quite different traditions and characteristics, composed of people who profess to be victims of the Land war that has been going on in Ireland for the past ten years. These gentry have for the most part recourse to heartrending efforts to make both ends meet. I knew a dudish sprig from one of the western counties (a sprig, by-the-by, belonging to a genealogical tree the origin of which, as the phrase goes, is lost in the night of ages), who paid his respects every Saturday evening to mine host of the Monte della Pietà, the Roman pawn-office, where his plate and jewellery slowly but surely disappeared, awaiting to be ransomed by rents that never came. One of the chief if melancholy characteristics of the Irish landlord colony of Rome is their shabby gentility. The male members dress in sombre suits that have evidently often passed through the dyer's hands, while the head-gear and dresses of the females, furbished up times without number, have quite too antique an aspect to command anything like respect. They live for the most part in cheap boarding-houses at the rate of four francs a head per day. Many of these boarding-houses are provided with little parlours, where a few of the 'exiles' meet to sip tea and discuss scandal on one or two evenings every week. All the chit-chat or gossip of the Irish, English, and American colonies is bandied about in those low musical accents peculiar to people who aim at being considered far above the common herd. The gentlemen twirl their mustaches at either end, or haul down their 'cutlets' (as sailors do their ropes) while bending graciously over the ladies, who are seated on rather seedy divans, and who simper and giggle and smile at the slightest compliment passed to their beauty – an article, by the by, which even to an Argus eye would be quite invisible, owing, I dare say, to the crust of poudre and rouge in which it is buried. There are, of course, a few exceptions to this general rule, but it must be in truth said that the matrons have a hard, severe expression of countenance, while the maidens are long, lank, lean creatures, quixotically attired and altogether wanting in that grace of manner and personal charms of the sex to which they belong. A man may run the gauntlet of a thousand or more of these high-born dames and damsels without the twitch of a nerve or a throb of the heart. If Dearmid's paramour were made of such clay as these, he would have never have been tempted to steal the lady from the arms of her lawful spouse.

Throughout the week the 'exiles' lead a dreary and monotonous existence. The 'fairer' portion of the community may be seen discussing small beer once in a while on the Piazza di Spagna, or peeping into milliners' shops in the Corso, while the gentlemen saunter into the office of the *Roman Gazette*, a dry-as-dust periodical, published in English, to consult the editor on the state of the political thermometer in the north-western corner of Europe. Some of these silk-stockinged oddities drown their cares at a grocer's shop hard by in a glass of Dunville or Jameson, the only thing Irish they care two rows of pins for, thanking Gilbey all the while for enabling them to quaff such a nectar on the banks of the Tiber. Like Alphonse Daudet's 'Kings in Exile', these lords of a bygone age are perhaps after all more to be pitied than absolutely condemned; for if they have committed sin, they have certainly paid the penalty thereof.

One of the most interesting Irish landmarks in Rome is the Church of Santo Pietro, in Montorio, an edifice overtopping the Janiculum, and commanding a splendid view of the Eternal City, as well as of the Alban Hills and their orange groves and beauteous vineyards. Montorio possesses a peculiar interest for the Irish visitor, for here lie the ashes of the exiled Earls O'Neill and O'Donnell, and here come in patriotic pilgrimages, week by week, Irish students or tourists, to pray by the tombs of those brave northern chieftains. Hither came also, now over half a century ago, a young and enthusiastic Hibernian, an alumnus of the Irish College, who was afterwards known to the political and literary world as Father Charles P. Meehan, the devoted priest who preached the gospel of Irish nationality in 1848, who consoled the dying moments of James Clarence Mangan, and who within recent years did justice to the memory of that high-souled, if unfortunate, poet. Here it was, amid the stately pillars of Montorio, one autumn evening, many, many years ago, he conceived the happy idea of rescuing from oblivion the annals that told of the career and vicissitudes of the Earls of Tyrone and Tyrconnel, as he stood pensively over the stones that marked the spot where their ashes lay. After frequent visits to the church young Meehan was informed that he might procure proper materials for his contemplated work in the library of San Isidore, where, as I have already observed, a very precious collection of Gaelic manuscripts was still preserved. Here he discovered a narrative of the 'Flight of the Earls', written in Irish by O'Keenan, one of their fellow-exiles. During the thirty years that followed, Father Meehan never ceased collecting all the necessary information for his projected volume, although he had had often to toil and labour under sad discouragements of many sorts, 'but always', as he says himself, 'with a desire to unearth a secret kept over two centuries, and to unearth the truth.' With this resolve he had recourse to O'Keenan's manuscript, already referred to, as well as to all the original documents bearing on the subject, still preserved in the State Paper Office, London, in Lambeth, and in the Burgundian Library of Brussels. Well and faithfully did Father Meehan accomplish his stupendous task, for his 'Flight of the Earls' must certainly be regarded as the most valuable contribution made to Irish history that has appeared within the present century. [. . .]

The slabstones that mark the last resting-place of O'Neill and O'Donnell would have been irretrievably lost were it not for the timely interference of Mr James Molyneux Caulfield, afterwards Lord Charlemont, and for the subsequent labours in the same direction of the Very Rev. Father Russell, of the Order of St Dominic. Mr Caulfield it was who, in 1843, defrayed a large share of the cost of the restorations, caused the epitaphs to be renewed, and the precious inlayings, which were much worn, to be replaced. Five years afterwards, in 1848, on the conclusion of the memorable siege, Father Russell visited Montorio and found several workmen engaged in flooring anew the sacred edifice. He represented the matter to the authorities, who at once had the Irish slabstones replaced in their former position. Some fragments of the ancient inlayings were in the possession of the Hon. Mrs Caulfield, Lord Charlemont's mother, a lady who belonged to the house of Tyrconnell. Some few months prior to her decease she directed Father Meehan to send the precious relics to the nuns of Ballyshannon, and have them inserted in the altar of the convent of that town, where they are still religiously preserved. It may be of some interest also to note that side by side with O'Neill and O'Donnell repose the remains of Beatrice, the beautiful and accomplished lady-love of the poet Dante.

The graves of the Earls are marked out by beautifully polished marble slabs, edged with marble pavements of white, black, and green, and having engraved on them the names, titles and coats of arms of the chieftains. [. . .]

Naples has also been the home of many Irishmen, among the more prominent of whom were Dr Madden and the Abbés MacCarthy and Campbell. Of Dr Madden, I have spoken already. The Abbé MacCarthy was in his day one of the most distinguished ecclesiastics on the Continent. He was born in Dublin in 1769 and proceeded at an early age to Paris, where he was educated in the University, and distinguished himself in all departments of learning. During the Reign of Terror, when a soutane was as much an object of horror to the Jacobin as a red rag is to a bull, MacCarthy had to fly in disguise from Paris, and took refuge in Toulouse. He was subsequently ordained priest at Chambéry, and became one of the first pulpit orators of France, despite the fact that French was not his native tongue. Great pressure was put upon him to accept the proffered See of Montauban; but his instinctive modesty shrank from episcopal honours. Shortly afterwards he joined the Jesuits, a company in which his high intellectual capacity had a congenial field for its exercise, and spent the remainder of his life in different portions of Italy. The Abbé died in 1833, mourned by thousands who admired him as a scholar and an ecclesiastic.

The Abbé or Abbate Campbell was one of the most prominent figures in the Court of King Ferdinand of Naples in the early part of the present century. Campbell was a native of the North of Ireland, and filled at an early age the post of chaplain to the Neapolitan Ambassador in London. It was while he fulfilled these duties that, according to rumour, he officiated as Roman Catholic priest at the marriage of the Prince Regent with Mrs Fitzherbert. He was subsequently summoned to Naples where he ingratiated himself so successfully into the good favours of King Ferdinand that he became all powerful and influential in Court circles. The Abbé mixed very much in society in Naples. He often sat at the table of the Premier Medici, hobnobbed with Lord Nelson, and took part in the dinners given by Lady Hamilton. He was, moreover, on terms of close intimacy with the then King of Hanover and the Duke of Cumberland, and was accustomed to boast that few of his humble origin could claim friendship with so many of the crowned heads of Europe. Dr Madden, who knew the Abbé in Naples, tells us that it was something more than amusing to hear the old man vaunting of his familiar intercourse with kings, princes and Ministers of State, and referring to them as follows: 'My friend Cumberland', 'My old acquaintance the King of Sardinia', 'Mio caro amico, Medici', and so on. When in 1821 an abortive attempt at revolution took place in Naples the government found itself obliged to exercise a very close surveillance over all foreigners residing within the kingdom, for it was on foreign gold that the malcontents thrived and flourished. Owing to his knowledge of languages and his devoted loyalty to the Neapolitan Crown and Constitution, the Abbé Campbell was appointed to the supreme control of the Post-office, where his duty was to Grahamise all the letters that passed through his hands. Sir William Gell, then a resident in Naples, protested against this tampering with his own correspondence owing to the delay occasioned thereby; but finding that his protest remained unheeded, he had recourse to sarcasm, and for some time adopted a formula written in very large characters at the top of the page of every missive of his, couched in the following terms: 'When the Abbé Campbell has read this private communication and replaced the broken seal, he is requested to send on the letter to its destination.' The Abbé's palace, the home of his declining years, was situated on the Capo di Monte, from which one could enjoy a splendid view of Mount Vesuvius and the beautiful bay at its feet. He died at an advanced age, leaving the sum of £16,000 to a nephew of his, who made ducks and drakes of the legacy some two or three years after he had come into possession of it.

Besides Dr Madden, there resided in Naples two remarkable Irish physicians, Charles Reilly and Fred Quinn. Reilly was the medical attendant of the Oxford family in Naples. He was an intimate friend of Murat, and took an active part in all the intrigues of King Joachim's Court, where he shone a bright particular star. He gave up medicine for matrimony in 1821, having married an Englishwoman, the wealthy widow of a Neapolitan, thanks to whom he lived in clover for the remainder of his natural existence. Dr. Quinn was about the same time a very eminent medical practitioner in Naples. He had been for some years the confidential medical adviser of Leopold I, late King of the Belgians, and the friend of boon companion of the leading litterateurs of Europe.

In a subsequent generation Denis Florence MacCarthy was a denizen of Naples. It was here he discovered that the famous southern bay, gorgeously picturesque though it was, could not rival his own native bay of Dublin. He had trodden the golden shores of Liguria and Sorrento, and yet green Killiney and Howth's brown sides had far more charms for the Irish poet. Some of MacCarthy's most graceful lyrics were penned beneath the blue Italian skies. It was in Florence he wrote his touching lay, 'Wings for Home'. La Spezzia was the creation of his 'Italian Myrtles' (suggested by seeing fireflies in the myrtle hedges), in which he quaintly but gallantly discovers charming types of ideal Irish maidenhood. There is in these passionate outpourings of the Irish bard a sweet, subtle flavour of the sunny South that renders them all the more beautiful and realistic.

IRISH FOOTPRINTS IN SPAIN, PORTUGAL AND CENTRAL EUROPE

Turning from Italy to Spain, we come face to face with other Irish associations. The connection between Spain and Ireland dates backwards for many a year. In days gone by Spanish sails were often seen around the Western and South-Western coasts of Ireland. Not only was there a thriving trade between both countries at the time, but many Spaniards settled down in Ireland and intermarried with the natives, proof of which lies in the fact that even to-day one may meet in the streets of Galway or in the Claddagh of the old town fair *colleens* who have all the raven locks, the olive-coloured cheeks, and the languishing eyes of the senorita of the southern peninsula.

Dingle, too, used to have its Spanish colony; while Spanish Island and Valentia Harbour still bear in their names close relationship with the chivalrous land of the Cid. Gaelic bards who sang of the lordly O'Driscolls and the martial MacCarthys, whose dominion ranged along the white foaming coast, were careful to speak in their verse of the 'Long-masted galleys' and 'noble fleets of wine' bearing down on the coast from the vineyards of Spain. Mangan, too, addressing Ireland, says: 'And Spanish ale shall give you hope, my dark Rosaleen', meaning, of course, by the word 'ale' the armed strength of the peninsula. Throughout the Penal Days the Spanish traders used to bring back with them a freight of the Wild Geese who fought and bled for the Spanish standard, or pilgrims bound for the shrine of Santiago at Compostella. Well and loyally did these Irish serve under the flag of the Philips. The Irish levies in the Spanish service numbered several regiments, one of which was known as 'Hibernia' and another 'Ultonia'. So true was the Irish heart to Spain that on one occasion a thousand or so of our fellow-countrymen who were serving in the English army under Stanley refused to turn their swords against the Spaniards in Holland. Nor were the Spaniards themselves callous to such manifestations of friendship and loyalty; for Spain was the first country that welcomed the Irish to its shores and provided them with the education denied them at home.

The first of the many Irish colleges founded on the Continent was that at Salamanca, established in the sixteenth century. After Salamanca we find seminaries at Madrid, Alcala, Valladolid, and Seville, where Irish talent was nurtured, and where it blossomed for many and many a year. These institutions were supported partly by the Crown of Spain and partly by the contribution of Irish merchants and of the officers of the Irish Brigade residing in Spain. The Irish College of Madrid was founded in the year 1629. One of its rectors was Don Demisio O'Brien, chaplain to Philip IV. It had a long and successful career, but it is now no longer the property of the Irish nation.

The Irish College of Alcala was established in 1657 by Baron George Paz, of Silveria, who gave it the interest of £5,768. It was incorporated with the famous university founded by the great Cardinal Ziminez, in which the grand Polyglot was compiled.[9] This Irish institution had for its object the education of students from the North of Ireland. Strict order, it seems, was by no means observed within its precincts, owing, probably, to the peculiar custom that prevailed, according to which the alumni were privileged to elect their own rectors – a procedure which produced much discord in the ranks. In 1729 the bishops of Ireland were anxious to cut at the root of these disorders by incorporating the College with the Jesuit establishment in the city; but they failed in the project. It was, however, finally incorporated with Salamanca in 1785, its last rector being the Rev. Patrick Magennis. It seems that the incorporation in question was not effected without a struggle. Father Magennis and a student named MacMahon barricaded the door and refused to surrender to the Spanish authorities. The mayor of the city, flanked by a posse of police, came to reinforce the military, but the brace of Irishmen laughed at the threats of the official dignatory, and defended the fortress till the door was broken open and the College was taken by storm.

Salamanca is now the only Irish College in Spain, and numbers some thirty Irish students, who attend lectures at the far famed university of that city. This institution has given eminent ecclesiastics to the Irish Church, prominent among whom was Dr. Hussey, who negotiated some of the terms of the Concordat with Napoleon, and who was, I believe, the first president of Maynooth. The Irish College of Salamanca, or, as it is officially called, the 'College of Irish Nobles', was, as the inscription over its gate announces, 'erected by the Kingdoms of Castile and Leon for maintaining the Christian religion in Ireland in the year that Philip III expelled the Moriscoes.'

Spain was the exile home of several members of the O'Sullivan Beare family. The chief of that sept, Donal Sullivan, took refuge in Madrid after the Castle of Dunboy had been captured and the national prospects in the South of Ireland seemed to be irretrievably ruined. He was on his arrival in the Spanish capital received very courteously by Philip III, who created him Knight of the Order of St James and Count Berehaven. Here he spent fourteen years, hoping against hope for an opportunity to strike another blow for the land of his love and ancestry. His death was a tragic one; for as he was returning home from Mass one morning he was assassinated by one Bath, an Anglo-Irishman residing in Madrid. [. . .] The chieftain's nephew, Philip O'Sullivan Beare, was highly distinguished among Continental scholars. Philip left Ireland at an early age, having been sent by his father Dermott as a hostage to Spain, where he received a very sound and liberal education. Having graduated with all honours at Compostella, Philip entered the Spanish navy, and became as accomplished a marine officer as he was an accomplished scholar. Annalists tells us that his cabin was well stocked with books, which in his leisure moments were his constant companions. It is recorded of him, too, that he used to write pamphlets and compile material for publication seated on a log on deck – even at times when the salt spray swept over the bulwarks and the good ship pitched and heaved in the storm. It was chiefly on sea that he penned his famous letters on the ancient Irish Church, which threw Ussher times without number into a towering rage.[10] The discussion between both savants was of a very lively as well as spicy character. Ussher upheld the theory that the old Irish Church was national and was not Roman, and that St Patrick himself was an honest Protestant gentleman in the broad liberal sense of that term. Philip O'Sullivan grew so highly wroth over these statements that he was tempted to ignore the amenities of polite debate, and hurled some very unsavoury epithets at Ussher's head. The latter, not to be outdone in elegant controversy, retorted by saying that O'Sullivan was 'as egregious a liar as any that this day breatheth in Christendom.' Philip O'Sullivan's chief contribution to literature is his *Compendium of Irish Catholic History*, written in Latin, and extending from the Anglo-Norman invasion to 1588. It was first published in Lisbon in 1621 and was republished in Dublin in 1850 by Dr Kelly, of Maynooth. Other minor publications comprising numerous traits followed suit, and established on a solid basis O'Sullivan's reputation in the literary circles of the Continent. His father and mother, who lived to be centenarians, passed their closing years in Corunna, where their remains and those of their son still lie interred.

Some considerable time after this date Madrid was the home of a Cork lady, who, curiously enough, was the widow of Muli

Mahommed, Emperor of Morocco, and whose salon in the Spanish capital was the rendezvous of rank and fashion, art and literature, for over a decade. The career of this creature is so interesting as to merit at least a paragraph at our hands. What her maiden name was has not been satisfactorily determined; but it is shrewdly suspected that the future Empress was a Miss Skiddy, of Castle Skiddy, on the banks of the Lee. It is certain, however, that she assumed the name of Thompson, owing possibly to the fact that that of Skiddy was a far from euphonious one. Miss Thompson was in any case the leading belle of the southern city. She had a pale, classic face, deep blue eyes, and a wealth of raven locks, which, added to the artistic mould of her willowy figure and the elegance and suavity of her manners, placed her above the level of would-be rivals, and threw all the local bards into ecstasies that found vent in the jingling rhymes of many a madrigal. A certain Mr O'Shea, a merchant from Cadiz, having visited Cork in the interest of his firm, saw the young lady and fell passionately in love with her. Whether she at first listened with favour to his suit owing to the fact that a wealthy husband was a fine 'catch' for a penniless girl like her, or owing to a nobler or more generous motive, the gossips of the day failed to ascertain; but it is admitted on all hands that the Spanish-Irishman, a tall, well-built, elegant cavalier, eventually made a deep impression on her heart. The result was that the lovers plighted their troth, and as Mr O'Shea's business engagements compelled him to return immediately to Cadiz, it was decided that Miss Thompson was in a month afterwards to rejoin him at Cadiz, where the marriage was to take place. The young lady embarked at the proper time in a vessel bound from Cork to Cadiz; but as ill-luck should have it, the barque was captured by a Moorish corsair off the Spanish coast, and the Corkagian damsel was made a slave and brought a captive to Fez, where the news of her wonderful beauty soon got bruited about, and eventually reached the ears of his Majesty, Muli Mahommed, who at once had her removed to his imperial palace. Her personal charms wrought such havoc with the heart of the dusky monarch that he laid his sceptre at her feet, and asked her to be his favourite Sultana. Her womanly vanity was highly tickled of course by this offer on the part of his Majesty, and she consented to be his mate. With that fatal fickleness of some members of her sex, she had forgotten the old love for the sake of the new. Flattered, perhaps, by the reflection that nature intended her after all to sit on a throne, and not to pass her life mixing sand with sugar and chicory with coffee behind the counter of a grocery store, she gave her hand willingly to the Sultan, and bore him in due time two pledges of her affection in the persons of Muli Ismeel and Muli Mahommed – a brace of Irish-Moors who were for years the pride and joy of the palace.

The fair Sultana was in very deed the queen of the harem. None of his Majesty's spouses had a tenth of the influence over him which she so cleverly wielded. To effect this, however, she abjured the Christian faith, embraced the religion of her adopted country, and gave over the European for the Moorish costume. The Emperor himself – be it said without offending the canons of good taste – had attached to his household a regiment of 523 troopers, all of whom were his own sons. The two young Irish Moors held respectively the posts of captain and lieutenant in the contingent. All was smooth sailing enough for the Irish Sultana during some fifteen or sixteen years. Morocco, however, was just then a country where political convulsions and court intrigues were the fashion of the day; and one bleak morning the Sultana awoke to hear the dread news that her lord and master was assassinated by a pretender who had seized the reigns of power and had himself proclaimed Emperor of the Moors. Before a similar doom could overtake herself she escaped in disguise from the harem and reached in safety the coast of Spain. The fair widow afterwards settled down in Madrid, where she lived with great pomp for many years. Eventually the authorities in Morocco offered her a home in that country, whither she returned, and where she died at a very advanced age. There is no record left of the fate that befel poor O'Shea, the jilted suitor. How long he kept murmuring to himself, 'Sister Anne, Sister Anne, is therc anyone coming?' will, I fear, ever remain a mystery, although if he happened to be a sensible man and had no relish for sickly sentimentality, it is probable that he abandoned all notions of the hoyden from the Lee in the love and esteem of a Spanish wife.

O'Finn,[11] a warlike Hibernian, must not be forgotten in our Irish souvenirs of Spain. This typical soldier was one of a number of Irishmen who were engaged or sold by the British government after the insurrection of 1798 to the King of Prussia to recruit the armies of that monarch; but having managed to escape from Ireland before 'delivery', O'Finn made his way to France, entered the French service as a private, and very shortly afterwards was promoted to the rank of commandant. O'Finn took an active part in the Peninsular campaign of 1811 on the French side. A squadron of British cavalry and a regiment of infantry having on one occasion fallen in with a troop of French lancers, surrounded the latter, who, being overwhelmingly outnumbered, were called upon to surrender. To the surprise of the British the response was a scornful refusal. A fierce onslaught followed, the lancers fighting with desperate courage, cheered on by their commander, who was so conspicuous throughout for his pluck and daring as to win the admiration even of the English enemy. Though the troop was rapidly decimated the remnant fought on animated by the wild valour of their chief, who, refusing the offer of quarter, was at last cut down. Falling from his horse, desperately wounded, he struggled to his feet, and facing the Britishers, he shouted in English: 'I am satisfied. Remember, I am an Irishman, and my name is O'Finn.' Whereupon he fell dead in the midst of his amazed foemen.

Of the other Irish associations in Spain there remains but little to be said. The Carlist insurrection, which broke out in the northern portion of the Peninsula in the opening years of the last decade, brought several Irishmen to the fore. With that fatuous loyalty to a throne which seems to be the dominant characteristic in the Irish nature, several of our fellow countrymen laid their swords at the service of that arch-humbug, Don Carlos.[12] Mistaken, however, though the motives of these gentlemen were, they conducted themselves throughout the campaign with the bravery and intrepidity of the race to which they belonged. Among the more distinguished of the Irish adherents to the Carlist cause I might mention Messrs Smith, Sheehan, Travers, Leader and John Scannell Taylor, all of whom, by a curious coincidence, hailed from the banks of the Lee. The Press on the occasion was also well represented by Irishmen; for in the Carlist camp there were no less than three Irish journalists – Edmond and William O'Donovan, both correspondents of two Dublin dailies; and John Augustus O'Shea, who was then acting as 'special' for the London *Standard*. There are even to the present day many Irish names to be met with on signboards in the streets of the towns and cities of Spain. The O'Reillys, the O'Neills, the MacCarthys and the Fogartys have still their homes and habitations in Seville and Madrid. One of the old race, Marshal O'Donnell, was for some time President of the Spanish Republic,[13] while other O's and Macs figured and continue to figure prominently in the public service of Spain.

Leaving Spain for Portugal we find ourselves in Lisbon, a city which was throughout the Penal Days one of the favourite places of refuge for the Irish exile. The Irish Dominican College of Lisbon was founded under the auspices of King Philip IV by Father Dominick O'Daly, otherwise known as 'Dominick a Rosario', one of the most illustrious Continental scholars of his day. [. . .] Father Daly was as clever a statesman as he was a proficient scholar. In 1655 he was sent as ambassador to Louis XIV of France to treat of a league of affinity between the two Crowns. The following year, on the occasion of the death of the Portuguese monarch, the Irish ecclesiastic celebrated the ascension of his son and heir, Alphonsus, to the throne with great pomp and solemnity at Paris. O'Daly died in the French capital in 1662. It may be added that O'Daly, who was offered the Archbishopric of Goa, but declined the promotion, was for many years the Vicar-General of the Kingdom of Portugal.

Lisbon was the last home on earth of the Irish poet, J. J. Callanan, the gifted author of 'Gougane Barra' and 'The Recluse of Inchidony'. During his residence in that city Callanan devoted most of his time to the study of the Portuguese language. Here he mused for several years, amid the ruins of the past, the great Roman aqueducts that still studded the land, and the quaint old fortresses that told of the by-gone domination of the Moor. They wanted, however, the legend and the song of his own country to speak for them in their desolation. His muse, strange to say, drank but little inspiration from the valleys where the orange and lemon trees stood, or from the hills where his eye could rest on plantations of vine and olive. Callanan, falling into feeble health, resolved at last to return to his native isle. With this intent he actually had gone on board a vessel bound for Cork, when the symptoms of the disease from which he suffered grew so alarming that he was obliged to give over the project and return on shore, where a few days afterwards, on the 19th September, 1829, he expired, in the thirty-fourth year of his age. Light lie the turf over the remains of this gentle bard under the blue skies of Portugal!

Coimbra, in Portugal, is known in Irish annals as the town where Dr Doyle, the illustrious 'J. K. L.', spent his student days and where he acquired much of that erudition which stood him in such good need in Ireland years subsequently in his battle with bigotry and intolerance.[14] The College de Graca, of which he was an alumnus, was annexed to the great Alma Mater of Coimbra, and went by the name of the 'Little University'. Doyle eventually, however, succeeded in forcing the portals of the big university itself, where many of his countrymen before his day were educated, among them being Archbishop Talbot, the spiritual adviser to the Infanta prior to her marriage with Charles II, and Father Luke Wadding. [. . .] Coimbra was at the time the most celebrated university on the Continent. It was most difficult to obtain a degree there, while the course extended to fifteen years. There were other Irishmen besides Doyle just then attending the lectures – Clayton, Hanlon, McDermott and others who afterwards became more or less distinguished divines in the Church in Ireland. Doyle had been one year in Coimbra when, in November, 1807, Spain and Portugal were invaded by Napoleon. In July, 1808, Sir Arthur Wellesley was despatched with a goodly army to drive, if possible, the French Emperor from the Peninsula. The students of Coimbra were enrolled against the French. Doyle, it seems, displayed much of what is called 'loyalty', was drilled, shouldered his musket, and went on guard. [. . .] The young Irishman fought through the campaign and eventually returned to Ireland in the closing days of 1808. [. . .]

Würzburg, the capital of the Bavarian Province of Lower Franconia, holds the ashes of the Irishman, St Kilian, the first apostle and founder of its Episcopal See. On the 7th, 8th and 9th July, the Saint's fete is celebrated.[15] Last July, on the occasion of the twelfth centenary of his martyrdom the city was most elaborately decorated, every street was spanned with triumphal arches, and the bells rang joyously, while in the Royal Theatre *tableaux vivants* were given representing various scenes from the life of St Kilian. Prelates, members of the Theological Faculty of the University, the Government and city officials in their robes, and deputations from the various schools formed a procession in honour of the centenary. St Kilian's body reposes in the crypt of his church in the town.

Dr Stein is the present occupant of the See, and is the eighty-sixth successor of St Kilian.

In Prussia, particularly during the last century, the tallest and the best built soldiers in the army were Irishmen. Ireland could at one time boast of claiming as her sons one-third of the body-guard of Frederick the Great. That monarch had a particular fancy for the companionship of noted writers, and of tall men. He admired physique as he admired intellectuality. The garrison of his palace were composed of troops among whom a man six feet high would be considered a pigmy. He had his agents all over Europe recruiting for this colossal battalion. Germany and Poland used to supply his Majesty with a fair proportion of these giants; but, proportionately speaking, Ireland carried off the cake. Mountaineers from Slievenamon or Cairn Tuathal, whose arms, as Lefanu put it, 'were as round as other men's thighs', took service under the standard of the illustrious monarch, and were in the Court gardens of Berlin during recreation hours, the centre of many an admiring circle of the high-born dames and damsels of the city. 'As fine a man as an Irishman' passed in the German language into a proverb in view of these Titans, the girth of whose chests was in mathematical proportion to the stature of their frames. Voltaire himself, full of gall and wormwood though his soul was against the Irish, had to confess to his Majesty: 'Sire, the race of giants who scaled the skies is not yet extinct, for in these Irish before me I can see their descendants!'

Austria, too, has had many eminent Irishmen in her service. Count Taaffe, the present premier, is the scion of a family that has given many members to the government and to the diplomatic corps of that nation. Nugent of Meath was a field-marshal in its army. To-day the four officers of that army highest in command in Bosnia are Irishmen. The Governor of Livno is Major-General O'Reilly. The second in command of cavalry is Colonel O'Herlihy, and under him are two Captains O'Sullivan. One of the generals of brigade in the

Austrian service is Rudolph Oliver Swanston, who hails from Skibbereen, in West Cork. Others are, or have been, aulic councillors, the confidental friends and advisers of the House of Hapsburgh. When Maria Theresa of Hungary instituted fifty Crosses of the Legion of Honour, forty-six of them were worn on the breasts of Irishmen.

One of the foremost figures in the military history of Russia is that of Field Marshal Count Peter Lacy. This typical warrior of his race was born in Killeedy, County Limerick, in 1678. On the signing of the Treaty of Limerick in 1691, young Peter, who had just then only attained the fourteenth year of his age, was an ensign in the regiment of which his uncle, John Lacy, Quartermaster-General and Brigadier, was colonel. Quitting Ireland with the remains of that regiment as part of King James's army, the juvenile sailed for France. Having landed in Brest he proceded to Nantes, where he entered, in the capacity of lieutenant, the Regiment of Athlone. He served valiantly in Marshal de Calinet's army in Italy, as well as in various campaigns on the Rhine; but when, owing to the Peace of Ryswick, the number of the Irish Jacobites in France was sensibly reduced, he left France to seek fame and laurels elsewhere. He was for some years a soldier of fortune, fighting at one time in Hungary against the Turks, and at another taking part in the guerilla warfare then raging around the Balkans. He eventually entered the service of Czar Peter of Russia, being one of the one hundred officers of Vienna who were engaged for his Majesty to discipline his troops. Step by step Lacy rose from a captaincy till he attained a post in which he was privileged to carry a marshal's baton. Annalists, generally speaking, give the Irishman all due credit for having been chiefly instrumental in reorganising many of the Russian regiments so successfully that troops who before his advent knew nothing of the art of war, were, under his tutelage, able to complete with the best trained men of any other European nation. 'It was', says Ferrar, the historian, a decidedly impartial authority, 'Marshal Lacy who taught the Russians to beat the King of Sweden's army, and from being the worst to become some of the best soldiers in Europe.' Having fought with ever-growing success in more than a dozen different campaigns, Lacy was in July 1723 summoned by the Czar to St Petersburg to take a seat in the Council of War of the Empire. In June 1724 he officiated publicly at the ceremonies attendant on the coronation of the Empress Catherine I. He was honoured by the new sovereign subsequently with the insignia of the Order of St Alexander and was appointed General-in-Chief of the Russian infantry. By a curious coincidence it was Marshal Lacy who, by Imperial command, expelled from Russia the Count de Saxe, the marshal of that name who subsequently led Lacy's compatriots to the battlefield of Fontenoy. After numberless engagements against the Turks, Tartars and Swedes, and having won higher distinctions than any officer in the empire, Lacy retired to his estates in Livonia, of which he had previously been appointed governor, and here he died in 1751, in the seventy-third year of his age. Lacy's name stands to-day in Russian annals among the most glorious names of the marshals of the empire, such as for instance Munich, Keith, and Lowen Dahl. [. . .] Marshal Lacy's success in Russia shed an additional halo on the valour and prowess of those exiles whom barborous laws had ostracised from the land of their birth and patronage. Among the other eminent Irishmen in the Russian service of whom we cannot, through exigencies of space, speak at any length, were the heroic Browne, Field-Marshal of the Empire,[16] and Admiral O'Dwyer, who commanded the Russian fleet in 1787.

Among the distinguished Irish diplomatists on the Continent we might mention Marshal Maurice Kavanagh, the Chamberlain of Poland; Colonel Harold, Chamberlain of Bavaria; Patrick Lawless, who represented Portugal, and O'Reilly, who represented Spain at the Court of Louis XVI; Count O'Mahony, Spanish Ambassador at

Vienna. Speaking of O'Reilly, Napoleon I, on the occasion of his second entry into Vienna in 1809, observed: 'It is strange that now, as in 1803, on my former visit, I find myself in intercourse with Count O'Reilly.' The Count, it may be added, was one of those exiled '98 men who saved the broken army of Austria after Austerlitz. Forty other Irishmen took part in the same battle on the Austrian side. To add to the diplomatic list it may be pointed out that Nugent was Minister of Austria at Berlin, and Clarke, the Duke de Feltre, was Minister of War in Paris, Browne was Governor of Deva for Austria, Lally was Governor of Pondicherry, and O'Dwyer was Governor of Belgrade. The Irish chaplains in the European Courts were also very numerous indeed. Dr Plunkett, who was afterwards Bishop of Meath, was the almoner of the ill-fated Marie Antoinette; Father Conry was a chaplain of King Philip III of Spain; Father Talbot was one of the almoners to the Infanta of Portugal; Father Gerard Robinson, an alumnus of Salamanca, was a prominent figure in the Court of Madrid; Father Archer, the Jesuit, was confessor to the Archduke of Austria; Father Bonaventure Baron, of Clonmel, was the historiographer of the Grand Duke of Tuscany; Dr Thaddeus O'Rorke, Bishop of Killala, was private chaplain to Prince Eugene of Savoy, while Father Ignatius Browne, of Waterford, Professor of Literature in Castille, was chosen as confessor to the Queen of Spain.

Many other illustrious Irishmen there are whose careers would be well worth recording – men who won fame and honour in every nation on the Continent; but the chronicler must put a limit to his pilgrimage and not trespass too far with the indulgence of his readers.

Chapter 4

Ireland and Europe

Some Concluding Remarks

I dare say that very few outside the circles of the inveterately prejudiced or the invincibly ignorant will have the hardihood to deny that Ireland has left indelible footprints on the Continent of Europe. A few months travel abroad, particularly in the Latin countries, would convince the most confirmed cynic that Irishmen can look back with legitimate pride on the history of their exiled forefathers in the forum and on the battlefield. It is quite true that – at least since the days of old King Daithi – the Irish never attempted to be lords and masters of any portion of the Continent. It is equally true that they never plundered the French or Spaniards under pretence that they had a God-given mission to civilise such peoples by pauperising them; nor did they flaunt a pirate flag on the high seas for the benefit of Irish Shylocks and the advancement of Irish commerce. The fact is that these Irishmen of past generations had such a large amount of what may be called spirituality in their systems that they very often sacrificed the material or practical to the ideal. They could fight for an abstract notion – for love, for glory, for liberty; but they never knew how to take up arms for a countinghouse or a till. They might under certain given circumstances develop into crusaders; but they never could become a nation of shopkeepers. Hence their feats on the Continent have not been productive of any material advantage to the land of their birth. If we were a money-making race, if our souls were confined to the pages of a cheque-book, we might sneer at the records of those soldiers and scholars of our race who forgot in the past to attend to their banking accounts. The stolid philosopher who botanizes on his mother's grave, and the scrip-and-bullion man whose Heaven is the Exchange, can see nothing heroic in the death of Sarsfield, or nothing useful in the labours of Brother O'Clery. The modern generation of Irishmen, however, clinging to the traditions of their sires, are still wedded to those Platonic ideas, the fundamental principle of which is that mind ought to be cultivated above matter, and that we have not been exclusively created for the worship of the golden calf. [. . .] If annals such as these have any moral at all, it must be that chivalry and intellectuality are qualities by no means foreign to the Irish character. [. . .]

Before concluding this series it may be appropriate to observe that the record, however imperfect it may be, of *Irish Footprints over Europe*, conveys one great moral which should not be forgotten by the friends or ignored by the foes of Irish nationality. That a race so brutally treated by its taskmasters in the past, deprived at home of all means of education, should have left such a glorious record behind it in the annals of European nations; that it should have had its representatives, bone of its bone and flesh of its flesh, filling professional chairs in the greatest of continental universities, marshals and generals at the head of continental armies, ambassadors in continental courts, and governors of continental cities, more than abundantly prove the absurdity of the proposition that a people whose children could reach the highest rungs of the social ladder and could rule and govern abroad are unworthy of ruling and governing at home. That rank political heresy is crushed for ever in the light of Ireland's glorious history on the Continent. Nor let it be said that the last page of that history has as yet been written, for in the far foreign fields from Dunkirk, to Belgrade, the Irish scholar and the Irish soldier are still foremost in the paths of honour of glory. Though the tide of Irish emigration has for the past hundred years found fresh channels in America and Australia, it must not be forgotten that there are Irishmen and sons of Irishmen on the Continent to-day who have a great and an illustrious future before them; for there at least they have that free field for the exercise of their talents denied them at home by the grinding oppression of alien despots. As the Irish poet, speaking of these compatriots of his, says:

> In Northern Spain and Brittany our brethren also dwell;
> Oh! brave are the traditions of the fathers that they tell;
> The eagle and the crescent in the dawn of history pales,
> Before their fire that seldom flags and never wholly fails.
> One in name and in fame
> Are the sea-divided Gaels![1]

Appendix

The Muse's Hour: A Selection of Davis's Poetry Written on the Continent

---

LOUGH INE

(a lake in the vicinity of Skibbereen, summer reminiscence of 1875)

Azure blue's the summer sky;
The faintest breeze scarce ripples by;
Calm and still the waters lie.

No birds' cries the silence break;
No shrill sounds the echoes wake;
Not a breath is on the lake.

Nature sleeps on yonder lea
Her midday sleep mysteriously;
All is mute on land and sea.

And all around where turns the eye;
Mountains lift their crests on high –
Looming, threat'ning to the sky.

Reigns a rugged grandeur there,
And a beauty fresh and fair,
Growing – glowing everywhere.

Glowing in each shady nook,
Wearing e'er a gladsome look,
Mirrored in each sparkling brook.

Glowing on the rough defiles,
Circling round for miles on miles
Carb'ny's famed one hundred isles.

Shimm'ring on the pebbly shore,
Stained erewhile by Irish gore
At the sack of Baltimore.

Dancing on the waves that play,
In their wayward childish way
In yon Castletownsend bay.

Glowing, glowing, more and more,
Till a smiling look it wore
On the headlands of Glandore.

All thus it is on all sides 'round,
From hill to hill, and mound to mound,
This spot seems all a fairy ground –

Sward of veriest em'rald green,
Streams and lakes, whose flashing sheen
Lighteth up each gorgeous scene.

A gem set in a hidden mine
Where the light of lights doth shine –
Such art thou, O dear Lough Ine.

Something worthy of our love,
That a fancy might have wove –
Nay, a smile of Heaven above.

Calm and still the lake thus stood,
Resting in a pensive mood,
On the lap of solitude.

And when day had come to die,
On the hills and mountains high,
Where they mingle with the sky,

Still a peace reigns on the lake;
No birds' notes the silence break,
No far sounds the echoes wake.

And when ev'ning shadows fall,
Like a dead fun'real pall,
Spreading darkness over all,

Still the waters, ever deep,
Sleep a calm, unruffled sleep –
I alone a vigil keep.

Faint and fainter grows the light,
Till the last rays take their flight
At the presence of the night.

Lo! the moon peeps 'bove the hill,
And her silv'ry smiles all thrill
Thro' the hearts of lake and rill.

Breathless stillness hangs around
Each dale and rock, and vale and mound,
That stud this now enchanted ground.

Breathless stillness in the sky.
Where the stars gleam up on high –
Gleam and glow eternalie.

Breathless stillness – nay divine –
Where thy placid waters shine,
In the moonlight, dear Lough Ine.

PISA

Saw I in the town of Pisa,
Hidden in a nook of glory,
Four quaints sights that strike the fancy
With a holy awe and solemn:–
The Baptistery and Tower,
And the Church, and Santo Campo.
Faith hath crowned this mystic quartet
With a deep mysterious halo,
Like the hectic flush of scarlet
O'er the face, whose 'prisoned spirit
Plumes its winglets for a journey
Down the cenotaph's abysses.
Summer's handmaids robed the Heavens
In choice folds of azure lustre;
Piping song-birds thrilled the ether
With their dulcet dithyrambics,
As I sat one balmy evening,
Stealing from a dreamer's musings
Secrets of each stone and fresco
Looking from that mystic quartet
In the beauteous town of Pisa.

*   *   *   *

Tully's speech had no such music
Surging o'er the Roman Forum

As the diction, sweet yet voiceless,
Swelling in unmeasured accents,
From the choir of stone and fresco.
They were each a mystic gospel
Ringing in the ears of mortal.
They were all one living parchment
Where the life of man is written –
Not in letters cabalistic,
But in characters resplendent
As the sun-god in the heavens.
Toddling childhood is indited
On the base of Pisa's Tower,
While the Baptistery telleth
Of the nights of lamp-lit study
That we spend in preparation
For the ever growing fardel
Place by fate upon our shoulders.
And the church is the arena
Where we toil, and joy, and sorrow,
Till a grave like Campo Santo's
Stills our petty cares and turmoils
As a lullaby the wailings
Of an infant in the cradle.

* * * *

And while still the bronzed cupola
Of the Baptistery gleameth,
Like some fallen polished planet
Mirroring the saffron sunlight;
While I see the blushing marble,
Bronze, and gold, and quaint mosaics
Of the church in the Piazza;

While I walk beneath the arches
List'ning to the honeyed chorus,
Rising like a glad *Te Deum*
From the lips of plants and flowers
Poured upon the swelling bosom
Of each aromatic zephyr,
Strangest feelings ring their music
Down the cloisters of my fancy,
Like a roll of trumpets pealing
Through the aisles of San Pietro;
And I think that were it only –
For a deeply-rooted longing
Once life's phantasy is over –
To be cradled on the em'rald
Of the motherland that bore me
Far away beside an ocean
Where my kith and kin lie sleeping,
I should find it bliss ecstatic
To lay down my head, and slumber
Here where death looks like a vision
Grander than the lotus vista
Of the happiest of dreamers –
Here, where life and joy run riot
O'er the tesselated tombstones –
Lulled to rest by balmy breezes,
Drinking from the dewes of Heaven,
Heaven's best and choicest nectar,
With the shades of mighty painters,
Sculptors, poets and crusades,
Heroes of mind and muscle,
Keeping watch and ward around me
On the breast of Campo Santo.

THE MUSE'S HOUR

O'er sparkling leas I sought the Muse,
Where, half in light and half in shade,
Dawn stood, Diana-like, arrayed –
Communing with the virgin dews.

I sought her where, in languid swoon,
Day on Apollo's bosom lay;
I sought her in each laughing ray;
I sought her through each golden noon.

I sought her through the autumn grain,
Where Solitude its vigils kept,
And evening shadows 'round me swept,
But, oh, my search was all in vain!

And yet, when midnight dreams arise
To graft new life upon the old,
And Fancy's leaves their wealth unfold,
And Echo's ling'ring echo dies,

She stealeth down infinite space –
Unasked, unsought, unwooed, yet won,
To breathe her lips' fond balsam on
The growing pallor of my face.

I know not if her tresses be
Brown, auburn, golden-hued, or dark;
But, though I see her not, I mark,
That none is beautiful as she.

I fail to guess the why or how –
I only feel that, like the tears
Faith shed on martyrs' precious biers,
Her kisses rain upon my brow.

I only hear her magic words
Ring symphonies athwart the brain,
That swell into a gladd'ning strain
Like voices of orchestral birds.

And as she chaunts, the grim earth fades
Beneath the wings of sparkless gloom;
I burst the bondage of my tomb –
I wonder through Elysian glades.

Aladdin's glories on my steal,
Joy bids me welcome as her guest;
I rest upon her fragrant breast
I hear the bells of fancy peal

A *Gaudeamus*, loud yet sweet –
An angel-choir, whose trumpets ring
A march of triumph, as they sing –
Transfigured at the Godhead's feet.

Life's shadows vanish, one by one –
Death and its fears are trampled down;
The wished-for-goal is reached; the crown
Of Immortality is won.

'Not yet! Not yet!' – the mocking cry
Falls dread as doom upon mine ears;
I look around in doubt, and here
I see but Terra brooding nigh.

Where hath my beauteous angel sped?
The balsam of her breath has died
Like sunshine o'er a fairy tide:
The Muse's hour hath come and fled.

CHATEAUX EN ESPAGNE

Ere I drank the gall of ruth,
Ere I felt the smart of pain,
I built castles in my youth
On the sunny slopes of Spain:
Reared I domes and gorgeous halls –
Weaving from a poet's woof
Ivory gates and starlit walls,
Lustrous spire and frescoed roof.

Phantom thoughts the ramparts manned,
Phantom dreams sat by my side;
Love and glory walked the land,
Balmy zephyrs kissed the tide;
Sky had sun and stars from me,
Earth its fruit and golden grain,
Till I fancied I could see
Heaven in the land of Spain.

I had hosts of visions there,
Purpled with romance's gleams,
Bright and picturesque and fair
As the Pyschès seen in dreams:
Like the tints of Summer's sun,
Like the sunset o'er the main –
Such were all the dreams I spun
In the olive groves of Spain.

Luscious lips were cleft to mine –
She and I had rare delights,
Quaffing love's delicious wine
Through the aromatic nights:

Passion's torch and Pleasure's sheen
Flashed their fire through heart and brain,
While I kissed my ladye-queen
On the vine-clad hills of Spain.

Beauty sang, and I gave heed;
Friendship spake, and I believed:
Faith was then no broken reed,
And I listened undeceived;
Candour shone from ev'ry face,
Ere each heart had proved a vane,
When I slept in youth's embrace –
Cradled on the breast of Spain.

Mine were noble promptings then,
Sacred as the saintly dead:
I could trust my fellow men,
And I followed where they led:
Life was then no grinning death –
Hollow – listless – ghastly – vain,
For I had a robust faith,
Dwelling in the land of Spain.

But, alas for trust and truth,
Friendship's smiles, and thoughts sublime,
They are but the seeds of youth
Shed to rot in after-time.
Lips were false that should be true,
Comrades vows were vowed in vain,
And I felt that I could rue
All the hours I spent in Spain.

Wrecks and ruins are the walls
Of my castle on the shore,
Desolation stalks its halls,

And the wolf stands at the door.
I am bowed with grief and care –
Old before my time, and fain
Do I wish that I had ne'er
Been an architect in Spain.

Life is black with Pharisees –
I can see the gilded plate
Hiding nought but dregs and lees
In the poisoned bowl of fate.
Earth is rotten to the core,
Pests and simooms sweep the main:
I shall pipe my reed no more –
Fooling in the land of Spain.

TO K.M.M.[1]

O lady fair, if wreaths there be to weave,
One garland green I'd fain entwine for thee,
Whose leaves should blossom evermore. Believe,
These are no idle strains, as I would grieve
For e'en rhyme's sake to sing in flattery:
A tribute of my homage I would lay
At thy small feet, where in no worship mute
I wish, dear friend, that I could kneel one day
And breathe the burning languor of a lute
That longs to sing thy praises e'er and aye.

If, once or twice through changing seasons, I
Might know that I'm remembered still by thee,
My heart would glow as thine own summer sky,
Dear lady, where it swoons upon the sea.

SONG OF THE VETERAN REPUBLICAN

(*an episode of the Paris Revolution of 1830*)

I am old, *mes braves*, I am very old,
And my locks are very gray;
Yet I was a soldier, young and bold,
On that terrible July day.
Ho! then there was fire within my frame
And strength in my raised right hand,
And a giant's force and a Vulcan's flame
Enshrined in my battle brand!
For I hated the merciless *fleur-de-lis*,
And the name its standards bore,
While the soul in my body whispered to me:
I could die for the Tricolour!

'Twas the last of the three immortal days –
those days of the month of July;
I stood where the Vendome lifts its gaze
Up to the summer sky;
Around me the citizen soldiers slept –
Locked in the arms of death;
(methought that the Heavens above had wept
at sight of their gore beneath)
Alone I stood, *mes camarades*, then,
With my trusty falchion blade –
Defying the insolent Bourbon men
On the steps of the barricade!

Ho! on they came, like a rushing cloud –
The cavaliers of the throne:
I clutched my sword and I cried aloud,
And my voice had a mocking tone:
'My creed is the creed of Eighty-Nine –

Lisle's song is the song I sing:
There are nobler hearts in a herd of swine
Than in the lickspittles of a King!
So, caitiffs, come! Though you crush me down
O'er your coming disaster wroth –
I can laugh at your Charles's gaudy crown,
And spit on his purple cloth!'

Their tiger yells broke on mine ears,
As I stood on the barricade there,
And I bared my breast to their sheaf of spears,
And I struck in a wild despair.
Then the blood gushed out from each throbbing vein,
And the light paled in mine eyes,
While the darkness of death, like a counterpane,
O'ershadowed the summer skies.
I thought, *mes frères*, I had died the death
Of a soldier who would be free,
While a curse broke forth with my last fierce breath
On the King and the *fleur-de-lis*!

Next morn I woke on a hospital bed–
I started to life once more,
And I smiled when a Sister of Charity said:
'The Bourbon reign is o'er!'
But mine was the wrath of the stormy seas
When she added with gentle grace:
'*Roi* Charles has fled from the Tuileries –
An Orleans takes his place!'
'Ah me!', I cried, 'was my sword then drawn
In the blood-stained city-rings
To plant on the throne another spawn
Of Kingships and of Kings?'

I wept, *mes braves*, and the tears gave relief,
Though deep was my weary pain:
Now I nurture my vengeance, and nurse my grief
Till I stand in the gap again –
Till the tocsin tolls, and the flags unrolled
Will laugh at a despot's frown,
And the dawn of a better day behold
The ruins of throne and crown.
When that hour comes–for the freedom of man
You will fine one trusty blade
In the hand of the old Republican
On the steps of the barricade!

ORANGE AND GREEN

I care not what your colour be,
If but with outstretched hand
You pledge in mine your fealty
Unto our common land;
Bound one to one by love like this,
It makes no odds, I ween,
If yours may be an orange flag
And mine the em'rald green.

What wots it that we pray to God
Each from a diff'rent shrine?
You are as loyal to your creed
As I may be to mine.
Why should we wrangle o'er the claims
Of doctrinizing schools,
While aliens forge our country's chains
And Europe calls us fools?

Your fathers died on Antrim hills
That Ireland might be free;
Some of our sires were ruthless foes
Of Irish liberty;
All have faults and virtues bright
No matter what their creed –
A noble heart's the only hand
That shapes a noble deed.

The self-same sunlight fires our veins,
'Neath the same sky we toil,
We struggle 'gainst the self-same lords,
And till the self-same soil;
Then, brother, let the old feuds pass
From that brave heart of thine –
The orange lily be thy crest –
A shamrock sprig be mine.

COUNT CAMILLE'S BRIDE
(*a legend of the Riviera*)

Count Camille's heart was dark with ire and sombre jealousy,
For there was not in Carlo's land a fairer dame than she –
Than Marguerite, his peerless one, for whose sweet favours sighed
The serfs and *seigneurs* on the shore, the boatmen on the tide.

Where'er she passed o'er hill or plain with footsteps slow or fleet,
One hundred voices murmured low, 'There's beauteous Marguerite–
'*La Belle! La Belle!*' the incensed strains rang round the coast, while she
Lay languid on the sloping strand – went boating on the sea.

Count Camille's heart was sore at ease – a solemn oath he swore
He'd take his bride where men might not behold her beauty more –
There where the prude, grave, hoary oak, the beech-tree, and the yew –
The monarchs of the woods – have not the plantasy to woo.

He gathered Marguerite one dawn unto his lordly breast,
And, joyously he bore her to the prairies of the west;
There, where no serfs, nor *seigneurs* bold, nor poets while they sing,
Could tempt her heart to once forget its sovereign and king.

Alas! alack! the forest birds from herb and leafy screen,
Sang songs of love and tenderness, and called her 'Beauteous Queen!'
The very trees bent on their knees; and lo! in tones discreet,
The flowers murmured: '*Oh! la belle–la charmante Marguerite!*'

Count Camille fumes in dudgeon just as jealous lovers can,
For Marguerite the darling is of nature and of man:
The arrant fool – he knoweth not that Beauty, like the Sun,
Was made to shine on *all* alike, and not to dazzle *one*!

THE ADMIRAL VILLARET[2]

(Time: 1796 [Brumaire, fifth year of the Republic]. Scene: the Bay of Brest, where the French ships lie at anchor awaiting orders for the invasion of Ireland. Sole Dramatis persona: an Irish officer in the French army.)

'Twas a pleasant afternoon,
As the sun shone from the west
On the spars of the stately ships
Moored in the Bay of Brest;
The breeze to the northward blew –
Inviting us out to sea,

Yet the sails lay coiled, and slept,
And never a move made we:
The frigates floated upon the tide
Lazily all the day,
While he smoked the sweetest of sweet cheroots –
The Admiral Villaret!

How I chafed in impotent rage,
Cursing the caitiff there –
Cursing his icy heart
In a whirlwind of despair.
For oh! his ears seemed closed
To the voices that called him where
A hapless people lay
Gyved in the lion's lair.
I heard the shrieks of the pariahs
Break o'er the waves that day,
And *that* is why I cursed,
The Admiral Villaret!

The wails of the orphaned ones,
The widow's sobs and sighs
Seemed to invoke dread vengeance
Down from the watching skies;
The land of my fathers called
For relief from its dismal pain,
And my strong frame shook as I thought
That she called, and called in vain!
While a nation's fate and fortunes
There in the balance lay
A cloud of the daintiest smoke coiled round
The Admiral Villaret!

What could Hoche in his anger do,
Bound, as he was, in bands,
The tapes and the twines of office,
Wrought by mechanical hands?
And Tone's wan face grew very pale
As he sat by Hoche's side,
And watched the perpetual ebb
And flow of the restless tide.
What could we do but gnash our teeth,
And in muttered whispers say:
'The Saxon has found his staunchest friend
In the Admiral Villaret!'

Oh! the weary watch through the ling'ring nights,
The grief with no reprieve,
As we waited the word – one only word –
Each dawn and noon and eve.
Where be the manhood that cries
'*Vive de la France la gloire!*'
Hath a palsy cursed the limbs
Of the Paris Directoire?
Or else how is it we thus stand still,
While day steals after day,
And idleness makes its very own
Of the Admiral Villaret!

Shall it ever come – the hour
When our ships will cleave the main,
And the eyes of the exiles gaze
On their motherland again?
Shall these corvettes ever wend
To the North their missioned way,
And glide with a freight of freedom
Into beautiful Bantry Bay?

Oh, I hardly hope to strike a stroke
For that dear isle far away,
While a cheroot gleams from the sullen lips
Of the Admiral Villaret!

AN IRISH PAGAN ODE

(*supposed to have been recited by the last of the Brehons*)

Taramis, O Taramis!
We lift our eyes to thee,
Where the lips of the setting sun-god kiss
The waves of the golden sea;
We kneel at thy mystic feet
On the bouldered crag, in the lone abyss;
And though each cloud be our winding sheet,
'Tis meet
That our orisons loud
Should ring through each shroud,
Till thou hearest our voices, Taramis!
Taramis! O Taramis!

Taramis! O Taramis!
Gone, gone are thy pomp and might,
We can find no trace of the promised bliss,
We would have in thy Land of Light;
The swords of our scabbards rust,
Our chiefs are *banshees* white,
And our baal-fires run to dust
In the murky depths of night.
'Mid the whirl and rack of black, black storms
Where Time's dread ocean rolls,
A palsy hath shrivelled our hands and arms,

And sepulchres are our souls.
  Cloud and after cloud unrolls
  A pleiad of frowns and a demon-belt,
  While the lightning tells and the thunder tolls
  The requiem of the Celt.

* * * *

Taramis! O Taramis!
There be ominous signs that we trace
And looks that look amiss
In the lines of thy sun-god's face;
Yet we worshipped the Sun, and prayed,
While our Druids, in gold arrayed,
Made the oracles speak from the belted flame,
Kindled in awe of his mighty name;
  Erebus, drear and dun,
  Its terror of terrors brays
  In vain down the wasting years
    On our cold unheeding ways;
    For our sires were sons of the Sun,
    And architects of his rays,
    And thus – O Taramis thus –
    What can Hell be to us
Save a cauldron dome where never dwelt,
One soul of a true-born Celt?
 Yet now the Lord of the Days
 Hath a weird and troubled gaze
And he scowls from his palace of gold
On our dutiful worship of Him.
Would he too fain join the Christian train
Of the Monarch of Bethlehem?
  Say what is the meaning of this?
  Taramis! O Taramis!

Taramis! O'Taramis!
Save us from Fate and Doon,
The Scylla and Charybdis
That are dark with a hideous gloom;
Save us by Ollamh's faith
In the name of our Fodhla's wraith,
By the Conn we deplore for evermore
Oh, save us from living death.
Save us, as Daithi was saved,
While with heart of a lion he braved
The gleaming swords of ruthless hordes
As the lightning round him raved,
And he sped on high through their shafts to the sky
On fiery, intrepid wings,
To the throne where now, with thy star on his brow,
Sits the last of our Pagan Kings.
Bid the mountains fall on each bending head,
Wrap the earth in a lurid blaze,
We would rather, O God be dead – dead – dead
Than live through these godless days;
For Death would be bliss
To a life like this
O mighty Taramis.

Notes

INTRODUCTION

1 Cork County Library, family tree of Fr Charles Davis; National Library of Ireland, baptismal record of Eugene Davis; *Eagle and Cork County Advertiser*, 11 Dec. 1897, 1 Jan. 1898; Rev. W. Holland, *History of West Cork* (Skibbereen, 1949), pp. 330–1; Seamus Fitzgerald, *Mackerel and the Making of Baltimore, Co. Cork* (Dublin, 1999), p. 11.

2 Richard Ellman, *James Joyce* (New York, 1959), pp. 129–31. Details of the Casey brothers' financial affairs can be found in Patrick Casey's correspondence in Trinity College, Dublin, James Stephens papers (within the Michael Davitt papers).

3 *Shamrock*, 4 Nov. 1876. This article appeared as part of his year-long series, 'Hours with Irish Poets'. Owen McGee, 'Eugene Davis', *Journal of the Cork Historical and Archaeological Society* (2004).

4 Mark Ryan, *Fenian Memories* (Dublin, 1945), p. 92. Reputedly, most of the editorials were written by William O'Brien MP, the editor of the suppressed Dublin edition, and smuggled out of Kilmainham jail

5 For the Parisian intrigues of British intelligence and Pigott, see Owen McGee, *The IRB: from the Land League to Sinn Féin* (Dublin, 2005), pp. 124–7; Christy Campbell, *Fenian Fire* (London, 2002), *The Maharajah's Box* (London, 2000). Michael Davitt wrote critically about Casey and Davis's activities in Paris in his *Fall of Feudalism* (New York, 1904), but later admitted to Michael MacDonagh (a friend of both Davitt and Davis) that he had got many things wrong, particularly about Davis and his moral character. University College Dublin, Desmond Ryan papers, Michael MacDonagh to Desmond Ryan, 8 Nov. 1937.

6 Janick Julienne, 'La question Irlandaise en France de 1860 à 1890' (PhD thesis, University of Paris VII, 1997), pp. 400–3.

7 Eugene Davis, *A Vision of Ireland and Other Poems* (Dublin, 1889), pp. 29–30
8 *Shamrock*, 3 Feb. 1877.
9 'Hours with Irish poets', *Shamrock*, 9 June 1877. Curiously, the verse by French and German romantic poets that he translated at this time for the *Shamrock* was predominantly militarist in tone, although his favourite French poet was Alfred de Musset (1810–57), who did not write such verse.
10 *Eagle and Cork County Advertiser*, 1 Jan. 1898 (obituary). T. D. Sullivan was quoted in this obituary describing Davis as 'a poet of conspicuous merit'.
11 Julienne, 'La question Irlandaise', pp. 339–43.
12 Andrew Russell St Ritsch (ed.), *Lays and Lyrics of the Pan-Celtic Society* (Dublin, 1889), pp. 73–4.
13 W. P. Ryan, *The Irish Literary Revival* (London, 1894), pp. 30, 45, 48–9.
14 Ryan, *Fenian Memories*, p. 92. A chivalric love poem by Davis, 'My Lady', was published by the *Dublin University Review* in April 1886. Though very proud of being from Cork, Davis considered that his family, like those of Thomas and Francis Davis, was of the 'purely Celtic . . . Cymric race' and this helped ensure that they could identify fully with Irish thought in their writings. 'Hours with Irish poets', *Shamrock*, 2 June 1877.
15 'Hours with Irish Poets', *Shamrock*, 16 June 1877 (concluding article of series).
16 'Owen Roe', *Reliques of John K. Casey, 'Leo'* (Dublin, 1878), pp. 1–2, 47–8, 53–4.
17 Davis wrote some fiction as a youth. A couple of humorous short stories by him were published by the *Irishman* during 1880, and the following year it published (in serial form) a melodramatic novel he wrote entitled *The True Love and the False*. This described a fictitious Irish artist's involvement in the Belgian struggle for independence during 1830. It was well written, but otherwise unremarkable.
18 *Pilot* (Boston), 25 Dec. 1897; *Eagle and Cork County Advertiser*, 1 Jan. 1898 (obituary, including extract of *Cork Examiner*); D. J. O'Donoghue, *The Poets of Ireland* (2nd edn, Dublin, 1912), p. 99; W. Stapleton, 'Eugene Davis: the Cork poet and journalist', *Cork Examiner*, 2 Jan. 1937.
19 The exact parameters of Davis's continental tour are unknown. It is known he lived for a time in Brussels during 1885 and Lausanne, Switzerland during 1886 and visited northern Italy and Rome, but it is possible that he did not visit Spain and Portugal at all.

CHAPTER I BELGIUM

1 An important synod of the Irish Catholic bishops was held in Kilkenny in 1627, although the 'Catholic Confederation', which Davis seems to be referring to here, was not established until October 1642.

2 Henry St John, Viscount Bolingbroke (1678–1751), a leading English Tory politician who fled to France in 1714 due to his Jacobite sympathies, wrote influential works such as *Letters on the Study of History* and *The Idea of a Patriot King*.

3 This could well have been Davis himself who, reputedly, was 'expelled' from Louvain, hence his relocation to Paris.

4 Peter Abelard (1079–1142), a brilliant but controversial twelfth-century philosopher and theologian.

5 He was castrated by the angry relatives of a young woman with whom he had a lasting relationship after it was discovered that they had had a child together.

6 Cornelius a Lapide (1567–1637), Flemish Jesuit and author of many works on the New Testament that were later translated into many languages and proved popular with both Catholic and Protestant theologians.

7 The revolutionary politician, the Marquis de Condorcet (1743–94), wrote works of philosophy asserting his belief in the perfectibility of man. The *Encyclopaedia* was a major work of the Enlightenment. It was edited chiefly by the philosopher Denis Diderot (1713–84), who was considered by contemporaries to be a controversial, anti-Christian figure.

8 Beauchamp Bagenal (1741–1802), a socialite from a wealthy Catholic family in Carlow, during his youth he had to sell much of his property to pay the costs incurred by his lengthy 'Grand Tour of Europe'. He later became an MP for his home county and an associate of Henry Grattan.

9 John Augustus O'Shea (1839–1905), a very well-travelled international correspondent for various newspapers, he was the author of several books and a well-known bohemian, wit and conversationalist. He was born in Nenagh and died in London.

10 Muslim.

11 Victor de Buck (1817–76), Flemish Jesuit. Bollandists are groups of Jesuit scholars who compile works of hagiography and seek to continue the same literary tradition.

12 'I shall not wholly die' (Horace).

13 The identity of this 'Professor O'Halloran' is unknown, but he was possibly a relative of the well-known figure of Sylvester O'Halloran (1728–1807),

a surgeon and historian, who was born in Caherdavin, County Clare. Sylvester's father, Michael, was a very prosperous Catholic farmer, while at least one of his sons was a successful businessman in Limerick city.

14 The pen name of Errijck de Put (1574–1646), a Belgian, best known today as a humanist, philologist and encyclopædist.

15 The pen name of Josse Lips (1547–1606), Dutch humanist and philologist.

16 During 1634 General Thomas Preston raised a regiment of 2,400 men in Ireland for the services of Philip IV of Spain and the following June they played an important role in relieving a siege of Louvain, attempted by a large French–Dutch army of 50,000 men .

17 A piece of contemporary Irish slang, which was particularly popular in Irish Republican Brotherhood circles.

18 Georges Boulanger (1837–91) was a well-known Brigadier-General in the French army and a very opportunistic politician. He sided initially with the republicans and during 1886, as Minister for War, attempted to remove all royalists from the officer-corps of the army. Upon the fall of the Ferry government in May 1887, he lost some political footing and so began siding with Bonapartist right-wing imperialists in an attempt to get back into power. He formed the 'League of Patriots' to champion their calls for a stronger, more authoritarian French government. Boulanger was seen as a military hero who could possibly avenge France's defeat by the Prussians in 1870. At the time of Davis's writing (1888) he was very popular, at least in Paris, and it was widely expected he might attempt to overthrow the weak republican government. In January 1889, however, he fled the country after failing to go through with a planned *coup d'état*. He was subsequently condemned by a French court for treason and, two years later, shot himself over the grave of his mistress in Brussels.

19 Literally meaning, 'wonderful to tell'.

20 The Battle of Fontenoy was between the British and the French (11 May 1745). An Irish brigade fought with the French, who were victorious.

21 Patrick Sarsfield, Earl of Lucan, brigadier-general in the army of James II, best known for his efforts to defend Limerick against a Williamite force during 1690–1. After the Treaty of Limerick, he and other Irish officers were allowed to leave for France, where they joined the Irish Brigade in the French army.

22 Davis once wrote a poem on Bruges, describing this characteristic of the city, although it was not one of his better efforts. Eugene Davis, *A Vision of Ireland and Other Poems* (Dublin, 1889), pp. 44–7.

23 'Carillon', from *The Belfry of Bruges and Other Poems* (New York, 1846), by Henry Wadsworth Longfellow (1807–82).

24 Kilkenny

25 The congregation was to be revived some years after and, after serving briefly as a home for refugees during the First World War, fled Ypres. R. B. O'Brien (ed.), *The Irish Nuns at Ypres: An Episode of the War* (New York, 1915). It later relocated to Kylemore Abbey, County Galway.

26 Many Irish soldiers, including Murrough O'Brien, served as officers in the English army under the Duke of Marlborough at the battle of Ramillies (23 May 1706), while others, such as Eugene O'Keane, served as officers in the French army under Villeroy. The English won the battle.

27 Henry Sheares (1753–98), the son of a wealthy MP, was a United Irishman from Cork who became a Jacobin after visiting Paris in 1792.

28 Two valleys in this region of Belgium.

29 Thomas Moore (1779–1852), Dublin-born poet best known for the *Moore Melodies*.

30 Alexandre Dumas (1802–70), French novelist and playwright, best known for novels such as *The Count of Monte Cristo* and *The Three Musketeers*.

31 The Battle of Fontenoy between the British and the French (11 May 1745). An Irish brigade fought with the French, who were victorious.

32 Cornelius Jansen (1585–1638), theologian, questioned the Catholic Church's interpretation of the writings of St Augustine and supported the theory of predestination. He won many followers in France, resulting in a long-lasting split within the French Catholic Church.

33 The family of Donal O'Sullivan Beare (1550–1618) of Beare, County Cork, who organised a rebellion against English rule, took part in the battle of Kinsale (1601) and fled the country with many others after his last stronghold, Dunboy Castle, fell to the English the following year.

34 William Thomas Stead (1849–1912), an outspoken English Liberal journalist and friend of Gladstone, he campaigned against suggestive literature and became famous during 1885 after highlighting the existence of an extensive slave trade, as well as many underground prostitution rings, in London. Known as an evangelical Christian on both sides of the Atlantic, he became a prolific author, was nominated for the Nobel Peace Prize in 1903 and died on board the *Titanic*.

35 The subject of Thomas Moore's melody, 'Lesbia hath a beaming eye'.

CHAPTER 2 NORTHERN FRANCE

1 Davis almost certainly did not check such records. Modern-day Irish historians estimate that, in total, probably about 60,000 Irishmen enrolled in the French army during the 17th and 18th centuries *combined*. This would seem a far more realistic figure, considering that the entire population of Ireland for most of this period was only about 2 million people. Nicholas Canny (ed.), *Europeans on the Move: Studies in European Migration, 1500–1800* (Oxford, 1994), pp. 125–6.

2 A tragic novel by Johann Wolfgang von Goethe (1749–1832), published in 1774 and a bestseller in its day. The novel takes the form of a series of letters by a highly sensitive young poet to a friend about his unrequited love for a girl. Ultimately, in his despair, he commits suicide, as did many impressionable German young men after reading the novel, because they felt they could identify completely with Werther's sense of hopelessness. Curiously the French composer Jules Massenet (1842–1912) was writing the opera *Werther* at the time Davis's book was published.

3 The Duke of Portland (W. H. C. Bentinck), a Whig, served twice as prime minister and was home secretary with charge of Irish affairs from 1794–1801, while Charles Fox, a noted Whig parliamentary speaker and supporter of Portland, served three terms as foreign secretary.

4 A prolific Algerian-born poet, novelist and playwright, Jean Richepin (1849–1926) achieved fame in France after being imprisoned for causing offence to public morals following the publication of his first volume of verse, *Chanson des Geaux* (1876), or 'the song of tramps'. Over the next 25 years he published five more volumes of verse in a somewhat similar vein.

5 Benjamin Disraeli (1804–81), first Earl of Beaconfield, Tory prime minister 1874–80, author of several novels.

6 A leading Parisian daily newspaper, which still exists.

7 Boulanger.

8 The first state theatre of France, it was established in the seventeenth century and is still in operation today.

9 Probably the least known of these four playwrights today, Victorien Sardou (1831–1908) wrote comedies and historical dramas. His melodrama, *Tosca*, was later used by Puccini as the basis of his well-known opera of the same name.

10 Alexandre Dumas (1824–95), dramatist and son of the famous novelist of the same name.

11 Possibly another reference to Sarah Bernhardt (1844–1923), although she was already a world-famous actress by the 1880s.

12 A French actress at the height of her success during 1888 but known to the public only by her stage name.
13 One of two brothers, well-known in Paris at that time as both actors and singers.
14 A nickname for the area between the Place de la Concorde and Arc du Triomphe, meaning principally the Champs Elysées itself.
15 Louis-Antoine de Noailles (1651–1729), a major figure in the history of French Catholicism, he served for very many years as the archbishop of Paris and was made a cardinal in 1700. He defended the Jansenists against Jesuit attacks and opposed an important papal bull of 1713, yet remained loyal to Rome. He was well known for selling much of his personal property to aid famine victims and for redecorating Notre Dame Cathedral.
16 The Battle of Fontenoy between the British and the French (11 May 1745). Lally led an Irish brigade that fought with the French, who were victorious.
17 Meaning James II.
18 This was John Patrick Leonard (1814–89), a Cork-born professor of English in the Sorbonne. He discovered the grave in 1879 and arranged the removal of her remains the following year. Mark Ryan, *Fenian Memories* (Dublin, 1945), pp. 94–7.
19 Frances O'Hagan of Glenaveena, Howth, County Dublin. She was the daughter of Thomas O'Hagan, who served as lord chancellor of Ireland in 1865, and the wife of John O'Hagan (1822–90), a justice of the high court, author of several scholarly works and founder of the Statistical and Social Inquiry Society of Ireland (1847). He resided in Paris during the early 1850s and knew several Irish exiles of 1848, including John O'Leary.
20 This is probably a reference to Charles McCarthy Teeling (1855–1913), a grandnephew of Bartholomew, who worked as a Dublin corporation official, was active in IRB circles and was prominent in the Young Ireland debating society in Dublin during the mid 1880s, before he was expelled for continual harassment of a socialist speaker. He remained well known in Dublin nationalist circles and socialised occasionally with Davis during the late 1880s.
21 Davis is being selective with the truth here. Henri Clarke actually promoted the Irish Legion during Napoleon's reign and was simply ordered to disband the unit following the Bourbons' accession to the throne in 1815.
22 James Stephens (1824–1901), the founder of the IRB, who resided in Paris from 1848–56. He knew Byrne as well as Arthur O'Connor through his membership of the Irish Parisian Association, a short-lived club.
23 James Barry (1741–1806) was born in Cork but was best known for his paintings in England. He is buried in St Paul's Cathedral, London.

24 Daniel Maclise (1806–70), best known for his narrative pictures, was a prominent member of the Royal Academy of Art, London, and died in Chelsea.

25 Henry Jones (1859–1929), a widely travelled but often forgotten painter, his work has recently received reappraisal thanks partly to Brendan Rooney's book, *Thaddeus* (Dublin, 2003).

26 Edmund O'Donovan (1844–83), son of the Gaelic scholar John O'Donovan and a member of the IRB, he was a well-known war correspondent and went missing and evidently died while covering the Sudanese war of the early 1880s.

27 Archbishop T. W. Croke (1824–1902), a patron of the GAA after whom Croke Park is named, was an outspoken and politically active bishop who became a strong supporter of Parnell's party, particularly after 1885, but he withdrew from politics during 1891 after taking a prominent part in the controversy surrounding Parnell's fall.

28 Emile Ollivier (1825–1913) was actually a prominent republican politician for most of the Second Empire (1851–70) and did not agree to work with Louis Napoleon, or form a government for him, until 1869.

29 It appears he was expelled with only one other Irishman, and this was Davis himself.

30 1808

31 McMahon died in 1893, aged 85.

32 The identity of this man is unknown. It may be George Henry Moore (1811–70), a leading Irish politician of the 1850s and 1860s, who, in the 1830s, travelled widely, lived wildly and developed a great love for horses.

33 Charles James Patrick Mahon (1800–91) of Ennis, known usually as 'The O'Gorman Mahon', he was elected MP for Clare in 1830 but soon fell out with O'Connell and lost his seat. After many years travelling the continent, where he instigated thirteen duels and held several military positions, he returned to Ireland, serving as Parnellite MP for Clare (1879–85) and Carlow (1887–91). He died in London.

34 This is possibly a description of Davis's own social cohorts in Paris; the compositors in question quite probably being the Casey brothers.

35 O'Donovan later became an assistant-editor of the Land League organ *United Ireland* (Aug–Dec. 1881) before transferring to the editorial staff of John Devoy's *Irish Nation* (New York).

36 See note 26.

37 P. H. Sheridan (1831–88), native of Cavan and educated at West Point Academy, he became a US general during the American civil war and eventually was made commander-in-chief of the US army in 1883.

38 John Savage (1828–88), Dublin-born painter, writer and 1848 rebel, he achieved popular acclaim as a dramatist and poet in the United States during the mid-1860s, though he is completely forgotten as a literary figure today. A one-time president of the Fenian Brotherhood in New York (1867–71), he wrote a couple of nationalist history books, contributed regularly to the *Irishman* and often visited Paris, though remained, and died, in America, where, in his later years, he worked as a lecturer in English literature at Fordham University, New York, and then finally as a civil servant.

39 The Franco-Prussian war of 1870.

40 A French parliamentary election was due to take place in November 1889 but Boulanger had already fled the country in disgrace by then. What happened to Morphy is unknown.

41 Davis and the Casey brothers were foremost in organising the St Patrick's Day celebrations for the 'Irish-born' in Paris. *Irishman*, 26 Mar. 1881.

42 Davis himself was its acting-editor.

43 These activities are described in the editor's introduction, pp. 3–4.

44 Possibly meaning Archbishop John MacHale (1791–1881) of Tuam, one of the most notable Irish Catholic bishops of the nineteenth century.

45 Justin McCarthy, Lord Mountcashel, was lieutenant-general of James II's forces in County Cork, and left for France after the Treaty of Limerick, becoming a lieutenant-general in the French army and assisted in the capture of Heidelberg and Darmstadt. He died in the summer of 1694 from injuries.

CHAPTER 3 ITALY, IBERIA AND CENTRAL EUROPE

1 The Edict of Nantes (1598) was a French law guaranteeing religious and civil liberties to the King's Huguenot subjects, but it was revoked in 1685 by Louis XIV, who feared Protestants could be a threat to the integrity of the state.

2 The Lord Cloncurry in question was Valentine Lawless (1773–1853) of Blackrock, County Dublin and later Celbridge, County Kildare. He attended school in Lausanne around 1792–3 before returning to Ireland, where he became a supporter of the United Irishmen. His *Personal Recollections* was published in 1849.

3 Edward Gibbon (1737–94), whose famous history was published between 1776 and 1788 in five volumes, but this work was started in 1772, by which time he was resident of London, not Lausanne, where he had only attended school.

4 Dr Glynn condemned the papal decree of 1869 forbidding inter-denominational education, as well as the American Catholic hierarchy's

attempts to influence the running of state schools in New York, even going so far as to proclaim that the Catholic Church was an enemy to the civil liberties of the American Republic.

5 Meaning the nominal archbishop of the Turkish city of Ephesus, where, in fact, there was no Catholic Church at this time. Ephesus was the principal city of the province of Asia in the era of the Roman Empire and St Paul was the Church's first emissary there. Consequently, the Catholic Church always considers it a place of much significance.

6 Pelagius, reputedly an Irishman, took the view that salvation could be achieved by human endeavour alone. St Ignatius (35–107) was one of the founders of the church.

7 John Locke (1847–88) of Callan, County Kilkenny, the son of an accountant, was a republican who contributed poetry to the IRB's *Irish People* and was imprisoned in 1867. Later, in America, he contributed verse and fiction to various magazines before returning to Kilkenny to work for the *Celtic Monthly*, a literary magazine set up by the local IRB leader, James Haltigan, in 1879. His poetry was never collected in book form.

8 Probably meaning the Boston *Pilot*, edited by John Boyle O'Reilly (1844–90) and a paper for which Davis also worked occasionally.

9 Jimenez de Cisneros (1437–1517), or Cardinal Ximinies (pronounced Zim-in-ez), was archbishop of Toledo. He was a champion of reform within the church long prior to the reformation, and founded the University of Alcala to improve the education of clergy. The 'grand Polyglot' was the so-called 'Polyglot Bible', an attempt to improve the existing edition of the bible.

10 James Ussher (1581–1656), the leading Church of Ireland bishop and scholar of his day.

11 This may well be a reference to Edmond O'Finn, a Cork United Irishman, who attempted to solicit French aid for Ireland during the mid-1790s and after the 1798 rebellion fled to France, joining the army.

12 Don Carlos (1848–1909) was recognised as King Charles VII of Spain by the Pope (this was why many Irish Catholics felt compelled to support him) and declared war on the Spanish government in 1870 but failed to secure the throne. 'Carlists' were supporters of the claim of Don Carlos (1788–1855) and his descendants to the Spanish throne. Several Carlist uprisings occurred in nineteenth-century Spain.

13 Davis is mistaken here. The First Spanish Republic (1873–4) existed briefly during the Spanish civil wars of the early 1870s, while General Leopoldo O'Donnell (1809–67), Field Marshal of the Spanish Army, served three terms as 'President of the Council of Ministers of Spain' (prime minister) for Queen

Isabella II in the decade before his death. O'Donnell was the leader of the 'Unión Liberal' party, which had occasionally formed alliances with the Spanish republicans in the past, but he was not himself a republican. His son, Don Juan O'Donnell (1864–1938), as president of the Convention of the Irish Race in Paris in 1919, supported Dáil Éireann's efforts to achieve international recognition of the Irish Republic and, at the request of Eamon de Valera, was later granted an honorary doctorate by the National University of Ireland in recognition of his past services to Ireland.

14 James Warren Doyle (1786–1834), as bishop of Kildare and Leighlin, wrote several works demanding Catholic emancipation during the 1820s. They were published under the initials 'J. K. L.'

15 Annual celebrations continue to be held in Würzburg to this day. St Kilian (*c.*650–689) is generally believed to have been from Mullagh, County Cavan. He arrived in Wurzburg in 686.

16 George Browne (1698–1792), a Catholic and Jacobite from Limerick, served in the Russian army from 1730 onwards, was second-in-command to Lacy, and was made a field marshal after his service in the Seven Years War (1756–63). In his final years he was governor of Livonia (Latvia and Estonia).

CHAPTER 4: SOME CONCLUDING REMARKS

1 This is a quotation from 'Salutation to the Kelts' by Thomas D'Arcy McGee (1825–68).

APPENDIX

1 This was written for a Dublin friend named Marcella Magennis.

2 It was owing chiefly to Admiral Villaret's apathy and indifference that the French fleet lay so long anchored in the waters of Brest prior to its expedition to Bantry Bay. (Davis's note).

Index